CREATION WAITS

by Agnes Sanford

*"For the creation waits
with eager longing for the revealing
of the sons of God."*

(Romans 8:19 RSV)

LOGOS INTERNATIONAL Plainfield, New Jersey

All scripture is taken from
the King James Version,
unless otherwise noted as RSV,
Revised Standard Version.

CREATION WAITS
All Rights Reserved
Printed in the United States of America
International Standard Book Number: 0-88270-250-5
Library of Congress Catalog Card Number: 77-91883
Published by Logos International
Plainfield, New Jersey 07060

DEDICATION

This book is dedicated to
Edith Drury
with loving gratitude for
all her help.

CREATION WAITS

CHAPTER 1

We have a duty to the earth on which we live. We are like a farmer who inherits from his father a great area of fertile land, a land which can either become fruitful and beautiful with useful plants and trees that bring forth luscious food, or it can go to waste and be filled with weeds and briars.

The Lord of this great field, the earth, has ordered us to take care of it for Him until He returns. This includes not only a missionary duty to the people who live upon the earth, but also a caretaker's duty to the earth itself. According to the old story of Genesis, man was put upon the earth to "dress it and to keep it" (2:15), and when Cain slew his brother it was not only a sin against man but also against the earth. "The voice of thy brother's blood crieth unto me from the ground," Jehovah said (4:10). Moreover, the earth itself, being cursed by this sin, no longer brought forth useful fruit and grain but thorns and briars.

There is a connection between the earth and the people who live upon it. "They have made my pleasant portion a desolate wilderness" (Jer. 12:10). So Jehovah said to the prophet Jeremiah concerning the sins of His people.

1

What does this mean to us little people of today, who are not Jeremiah neither any kind of prophet? It means that we are to pray not only for sick or troubled people, but we are also to pray for the earth itself. This is a joyous thing! People may resist us; the earth will not. People may fail to be grateful. The earth will not fail, but will shower us with blessings if only we shower it with the blessings of God's love.

The reader has the right to ask how I know this. I know it not only because the Bible says so, repeatedly and in all kinds of ways, but also because I have tried it and it works! I challenge the reader also to *try it and see.* He will need to give it a sufficient try, considering carefully what part of "inanimate" nature to pray for, and how long to continue the prayer.

My own first real earth-project was the San Andreas Fault, a rift in the earth running north and south along much of the West Coast, and subject to disastrous earthquakes. I began to pray, with particular emphasis on the section of this fault in Southern California, that it might accomplish its work of relieving the tension in the earth's crust quietly, with sufficient small tremors, but without destructive earthquakes. To this work I was called, I believe, much as Abraham was called to leave his home and go forth to a strange land (Gen. 12 ff.).

The manner of my calling was as follows. Comfortably settled in New England, for many days I felt an unreasoning depression. My experience has been that such a feeling either means that I am "off the beam" in my own spiritual life, or that someone somewhere is urgently calling on me for prayer. I searched my soul for the reason for this depression and found nothing of significance in myself or among my friends or family. Finally I said, "Lord, *what is it?*" and listening for the answer had the feeling that it was not a person but a place that needed prayer.

"Lord, *where* is it?" I asked, and listened. There came to my mind the northwestern part of the United States, and it seemed that some calamity threatened that region.

"May I pray that whatever is to happen may be averted?" I asked, and listening heard a negative response. This prayer was too great for me.

"May I pray for it to be minimized?" I asked, and quite distinctly I heard, "Yes."

So for three days I prayed for the Northwest, for the land and area itself, and when not in active prayer I held it as an undercurrent to other thoughts. And then there came the earthquake in the state of Washington which just missed being a really destructive one. And my burden was lifted, for its work was done.

In due time my decision to move from New England to the West Coast was made partly because of the need of that which has become my greatest "patient," the San Andreas Fault.

However, I am not writing here in concern for western California. It is in concern for the faith of many Christians who are able to pray for the salvation and even the healing of persons but who are able to go no farther in carrying out the commands of their Lord to make this little earth into a kingdom of heaven.

Many Christians have given up the battle before it has even begun. They do not seriously consider the Lord's words concerning His coming again and the kingdom of heaven. They tend to fasten their eyes not on a saved and transformed earth with the glory of God shining beyond and upon it, but on the Great Tribulation, an event that is past. Not realizing that this actually took place long ago, they spend much of their time and spiritual energy praying that they may be able to endure it when it comes.

Jesus did warn His disciples of the Great Tribulation, and prayed for them that their faith would not fail—and it did not. They were persecuted in the most savage ways by the emperor of the Roman Empire. They were crucified, they were thrown to the lions, they were killed with the sword—and they stood fast.

They refused to deny Jesus as their Lord, and endured to the end. These first Christians saved the kingdom of God for us, and we stand, as it were, on their shoulders. So I am convinced that this terrific event is in the past, not the future! We are to rejoice in the faith of those martyrs for our Lord, and go forward and make this earth His kingdom. We are most definitely not to walk backward to another great tribulation!

Yes, there have been repetitions of the early persecutions, though none so severe as those which the disciples endured. There have been risings against the Lord and against His people in Russia and in China. How many more such persecutions there may be, like the aftershocks of an earthquake, I do not know. For it all depends upon us. According to the Bible, the Lord of the vineyard will be very cross with us if we let His pleasant pastures of the earth revert to a desolate wilderness on account of our lack of faith (Matt. 21:33-43).

Strange to say, this negative attitude is often held by the very ones who should be most joyously positive, since they love the Lord with their whole hearts—almost. I once knew a young woman who stated blithely that she needed a new pair of shoes but there was no need to buy them because Jesus was coming back in June, and then she would be caught up to meet Him in the air, and she would need no shoes. That was some twenty years ago, and either her shoes or her ideas must have worn through by this time. She thought, poor dear, that the earth was going to be destroyed by fire and all the bad people would be burnt up, which prospect seemed rather to please her, since Jesus would come again to this earth and rescue His own (among whom she was) and take them safely to heaven. Now there is something to this, as we know from the Bible, but apparently the time is not yet. I grieve for the lady's disappointment that the earth was not at the expected time destroyed by fire, but I hope that she has relaxed by now and has been taking good care of herself and her environment.

4

Others today also predict the destruction of this earth, and they are the astronomers, the ones who should know if anyone does. Astronomers read the signs of the stars not by fortune-telling but by a cold and rigorous study of those far-off suns, the stars, and of their rise and fall in other "universes," inconceivably far away. Men of science perceive by actual observation, not by theorizing or speculating, that stars do not live forever, and that ours is actually one of the lesser suns, or stars. They are centers of unimaginable heat, raging and exploding as they whirl through the heavens, and presumably, so says modern astronomy, they all have planets or earths that rotate around them. Neither scientists nor Christians know whether there are living beings on these other earths, though very likely there are. As a Greek astronomer of the thirteenth century said, to think that this earth was the only one that brings forth living beings would be like looking at a field of wheat, pointing to one stalk, and saying that it alone would bring forth grain.

In due course of time (millennia, not years) these stars or suns come to an end. Either they gradually burn out and lose their heat, or they explode due to the tremendous forces within them. If our sun should cool even slightly, we would quickly freeze. If it should explode, all its planets would be destroyed by fire. This event, according to astronomers, will probably take place in about fifty billion years. By that time the lady mentioned above will probably be quite beyond a need for shoes.

The reader may possibly wonder why a small, ordinary woman like myself should speak so earnestly of astronomy. I wonder too, for the Lord apparently put into my mind when very young a thirst for knowledge of the heavens. So I studied astronomy in college, and have kept up with its new developments ever since, all this with great tearing of hair and mopping of brow, for it is very difficult and I am no mathematician!

What is my purpose in citing these prophecies here? It is to say that there is still time to do what our Lord commanded: to take care of this earth that is to be His kingdom—and we had better get with it!

In other books on healing, I have suggested beginning by praying for small things in order to proceed to greater matters. And so I do now. Our aim is simply to obey our Lord when He told us to pray, "Thy kingdom come, thy will be done, on earth as it is in heaven." So we can begin by praying for the small bits of earth that we know, and for the creatures who live there, and for the crops that they and we need for sustenance. These are the old familiar prayers that we hear in church or read in our prayer books and Bibles, but we need to put teeth into them. That is, to make them work we must pray these prayers with faith that they will be answered.

We pray for peace on earth, and that is good, but do we believe that in answer to one prayer all wars will cease upon the earth and peace will reign? Certainly not, and we are right, for that prayer is too big for us. In order to bring the answer, we need to break it down to smaller components, just as in healing it is quite impossible for us to pray believing that all sick people will at that moment be healed. We need to choose a certain person, and to pray believing for that one until we see healing come.

Do not worry about this rather childish concept of prayer, for probably you do it this way anyway without realizing just what you are doing or why. Surely you have laid your hands upon an unhealthy rose bush and have lifted your heart to the Lord, perhaps feeling a little shy about saying, "O Lord, please heal this rose bush," but longing and hoping for it in your heart. Why anyone would feel shy about asking God to bless their flowers or their gardens or their fields I do not know, for the Bible is full of such prayers beginning with the first chapter of Genesis. Look and see! Go to church, listen and hear!

Recently I had dinner with my daughter and her family, and

exclaimed over the size of the red roses on her table. "That rose used to be a little squinched up thing," she said, using a word possibly not in the dictionary. "And one of my friends was in the garden with me and scolded me for letting that bush hear me say it had miserable flowers. She suggested that I tell it that it's going to have great big beautiful roses, and see what happens. So every day I've been doing that, praising it for the big blossoms it's going to have—and look!"

But roses do not have ears that they may hear! No, of course they don't. However they do have within them that same light or energy of God that He breathed into man at the creation (Gen. 2:7). Therefore even without ears they can catch the *feeling* of words, the energy released through words, and can respond to it.

You see, God is light! He is not an old man with a beard four feet long, even though Michelangelo could think of no other way to depict Him. Indeed there is no way to depict Him! Pure energy cannot be photographed or drawn, and God is not only pure energy but is the creator of all the light-energy from which all worlds are made. "For with thee is the fountain of life: in thy light shall we see light" (Ps. 36:9). The thing is inconceivable; it is stunning. Yet it is true. Science can give no cause for the creation of all worlds, but the Bible can. "And God said, Let there be light: and there was light" (Gen. 1:3).

From that light every created being or animal or object was created, and so the substance of every plant and animal and man is the original energy of God that we call light.

We have heard of people with a "green thumb" for whom all plants seem to grow. The power within them is not a "green thumb," but it is that light of God flowing forth on the thought waves of love to the plants which they tend, and to the earth itself, the creation on which we live. "For the creation waits with eager longing for the revealing of the sons of God" (Rom. 8:19 RSV).

7

While numbers of us are waiting for Jesus to come again in glory and make it unnecessary for us to buy a new pair of shoes, He is not likely to come because the earth itself is waiting for *us* to make it into the kind of earth whereon the Lord can abide to fulfill in it whatever is its divine destiny. When the eager longing of creation waiting for the revealing of the sons of God is satisfied, then will the Lord himself descend from heaven with a shout and with the sound of a trumpet!

While we are waiting for Him, He is in fact waiting for us.

What is the divine destiny of this creation? I do not know. The end of it is too far away. I cannot see it, but I know the beginning of it, for it is here, closer than breathing, nearer than hands and feet. It is that the love of God so fills us as to bring us bit by bit nearer to the destiny of man as described in the Bible: to rule over this world by love. As the end draws near, we are told that the wolf and leopard will lie down with the lamb and the little child will play on the hole of the asp (Isa. 11:6,8). There will be a natural bond of love that will more and more unite all sentient things, even people.

The end of this I do not see, but I do see the beginning. Not only is the light of God so present in my plants that people wonder what kind of fertilizer I use, but also this same light flows between me and all living things. In my early years in China I was terrified of dogs for they were savage creatures and were not discouraged from biting "foreign devils." This fear has simply vanished, I know not how. At first I noticed that if I were in a room full of people, and if the family dog came in, he would pass by all the inviting laps of cooing ladies and come and lie down at my feet. Now I find that if I walk up the canyon near my house about five dogs will "prevent and follow" me with every evidence of delight. And I enjoy it! One of these dogs, a husky, will stand on his hind feet, put his forepaws on my shoulders, and lick my face, and I accept it placidly, for he is my friend.

In fact I have a concern for all animals, and fear none of them.

8

A few days ago I heard the whirr of a rattlesnake in some dense geranium plants just beside my house. So I gave him the call of the jungle, "We be of one blood, thou and I!" (learned not from the Bible but from Kipling's *Jungle Books*). And I said to the bit of his mottled skin that I could see, "You are very welcome in my garden, but at your convenience I would appreciate it if you would move a little farther from the house. Okay?"

Apparently he did so, which proves nothing for he might have been planning to move at that time anyway, but I felt no need to run shrieking for an axe to attack him with. There was room in God's kingdom for both of us.

When bees or spiders come into my house I remove them gently, holding them with a bit of tissue and setting them down outside the front door. The only creature which up until this time has defeated me completely is the mosquito. This must be a weakness of my nature, for I know another woman of about my age who has acquired the victory over mosquitoes. She is a psychologist, though I doubt whether the mosquitoes understand that, but as she walks through her desert gardens and mosquitoes fly around her, she explains to them that they have their place and she has hers, and the immediate vicinity of her person is *her* place. If one of them lingers on her arm she points to it firmly and says, "And that goes for *you* too," and away it flies. She is writing a book about her desert home and the creatures around it.

Once I complained to a neighbor that the deer came down from the mountains and ate all the buds off my roses. "What shall I do?" I asked.

"Oh, my dear," she said. "Plant some more roses for them! For the mountains are so dry, and the mother deer are trying to bring up their young!"

I did plant the deer some more roses, which they seemed to appreciate, but it was quite impossible for me to grow enough roses to feed all the deer on all the mountains, so I meditated on the subject of praying for rain, that it might no longer be so dry. Now in California it is very difficult to pray for rain because someone always wants to go to the seashore or the mountains, and they do not want it to rain. However, most people forget that beyond the cities there are orchards and vineyards fighting to maintain life against the searing drought, and that far away on the mountains forest fires are spreading through dry underbrush. It is a strange thing about people: unless fires are heading toward their own houses, they often do not care.

At a time of great drought I was lecturing at Melodyland, a Southern California center for prayer and spiritual healing, and I presented to them the need of the land for rain. They saw the need, and then and there those thousands of Christian people joined with me in a faithful prayer for rain. No rain at all was predicted in the short or long range forecasts, but within an hour after this prayer great excitement broke out on the weather broadcasts because three different rain-bearing weather fronts which had not been moving anywhere began to move toward California, for no reason that the broadcasters in their agitation could find out. One front was in Mexico, but was far from us and stationary until the Lord called it toward us. One was in the East and one in Canada. All three moved fast and converged, and by noon the next day it was raining! It rained for five days and the drought was broken. Surely this was God's will, accomplished through the prayer of faith.

But why does He not simply do His will at all times without any regard to our prayers? I do not know. When I get to heaven I am going to ask Him. But in so far as I can tell from the Bible and from life, He wants us to grow up to become the sons and daughters of God, and He has given us this earth that we may learn from it. ''The heaven, even the heavens, are the LORD's: but the earth hath he given to the children of men'' (Ps. 115:16). Maybe God would feel unsatisfied in heaven all by himself. Maybe that is why He takes to himself the church, His people,

His bride. Maybe that is why eternity is not pictured as merely the everlasting glory of God upon His throne, but also as crowds of people surrounding that throne enjoying His glory, and adding to it by their own bits of light (Rev. 5:11-14)!

In the Presbyterian Shorter Catechism there is the question: "What is the chief end of man?" And the answer is: "The chief end of man is to glorify God and to enjoy Him forever." Not bad. But do we really glorify God when we use His power and thus bring about little miracles on this earth? Certainly! We are chosen for this purpose just as an electric light bulb is chosen to shine forth the energy from the powerhouse. Jesus is our powerhouse, translating the energy of God into terms of soul-saving and life-giving energy for this world. But just as a powerhouse cannot give light directly to the many homes connected with it, but must have the wires and light bulbs through which this energy is transmitted, so Jesus the Transformer needs us; God's power sent into the world through Jesus Christ yet needs us smaller beings to transmit that eternal radiance into the world, that it may become His kingdom. "Ye are the light of the world" Jesus said (Matt. 5:14), and again He said that we are the branches on which the tree of life is able to grow its fruit. "I am the vine, ye are the branches" (John 15:5). As a tree cannot grow fruit without its branches, neither can our branches bring forth fruit unless they remain tightly joined to the tree so that the life-force of the tree can flow through them.

On the occasion of the above-mentioned drought in California, I myself had been praying for rain, but no rain had come. The channel of my prayer was not big enough to end that widespread drought. But when several thousand people prayed with me, a broad enough channel was opened and the rains came. Some may wonder why God could not hear the voice of one person praying alone as well as He could hear the voice of thousands. He could, of course! But prayer is more than merely asking God to act unilaterally. Prayer is asking God to send His

11

power through the channel of our faith, that His light may shine through us. One light bulb may be a sufficient channel to light a kitchen, but many light bulbs are required to light an auditorium. Moreover, these light bulbs must be in contact with the current of electricity. Thousands of people sitting in an auditorium thinking their own thoughts do not make an open channel for the pouring forth of a miraculous power. But when they unite together, giving their souls to God as conductors, then the light that enlightens the world shines through them into His creation.

The needs of our earth are far greater than merely the elementary need of rain. The dangers that threaten us are far greater than the danger of drought. Greatest of all is the danger of the destruction of God's earth through wars among men.

There was a time some years ago when Edith Drury and I were in Paris where I had been asked to give some talks. We were staying with a hospitable French lady who was showing us the great sights of Paris. "In this street," she said, "thousands were killed in the war, thousands! In this street—oh, horrible, horrible—all destroyed, all, all destroyed. And now we shall have war again!" she cried, for this was just before what came to be called the Six-Day War in the Near East. "All will be destroyed! Your country will be brought in, we will be brought in—all nations—and we will have World War III!"

"No, we will *not* have World War III!" I said at the top of my lungs there in the streets of Paris. For a strange thing happened to me. I felt my spirit swept into a wave, a flow of energy from God. I was caught up out of myself, and the words I spoke were not my own, but were from Him. "Jesus said," I continued, "that if two of us shall agree on earth as touching anything that we shall ask, it shall be done for us of our Father which is in heaven. For where two or three are gathered together in His name, there He is in the midst of them" (Matt. 18:19-20). Now there we were in His name, we three, and there was the Cathedral of Notre Dame, so I said, "Let us go in and pray the prayer of command, that the conflict in the Near East should come to an end just as soon as possible and that there should be no World War III."

So we went into the great cathedral and seated ourselves in one of the front seats among people who came and went away again. I led the prayer, forbidding in His name that this war should become a world conflict, and praying that the water of life of Jesus Christ should fall upon it and put out its fires. As I prayed I knew that it would be so, and therefore gave thanks for it. The war did in fact cease in six days, and it is often referred to by that name, or as a "miracle war."

By no means have all people settled down and decided to be good. Where on this earth has that yet taken place? There are problems not solved and hostilities not softened into gentleness. But World War III did not develop, and I feel sure it was an answer not only to my prayers but to the prayers of many people all over the world. "He maketh wars to cease unto the end of the earth" (Ps. 46:9). So He does, if we have the courage to speak the word for Him.

Someone may think, quite naturally, "That is too big for me. I couldn't pray for anything so vast." Very well, let me suggest something smaller.

A few years ago just before Christmas there was a disturbance in the high school in the city where I live. All the details were not known to me, but a boy who happened to be black was lodged in jail overnight, and in the morning he was found, tragically, hanged, whether by his own hand or someone else's no one knew. The black people who comprise about 40 percent of the town population were, naturally enough, upset, and they showed it by thronging the streets and roughing things up, they and others who joined them. A few small fires were set and store windows were broken, with the result that nobody dared to go Christmas shopping. I would probably not have known about

13

this except that one of my best friends runs a gift department in her husband's hardware store, and nobody was coming to buy her truly beautiful cut glass and art objects. The hardware department was also hit, as were all the local stores which counted on normal Christmas business. All up and down the main street the music was caroling gaily over loudspeakers and the street hung with greens and tinsel. (Anything more beautiful than the backdrop of snow-capped mountains behind all these decorations would be hard to imagine.) And there stood the clerks forlornly behind their counters, selling almost nothing.

So the three of us—the seller of cut glass, Edith and I—convened a prayer group of ourselves and three black friends. One was my domestic helper, a very real friend. Another was one of the altos in our church choir, and the third was a black lady for whom the hardware store lady had done some decorating. We met to pray for the peace of our city. And our prayer included giving thanks for peace, imagining all animosity and fear forgotten and the stores full of people happily shopping for Christmas.

So it was! The very next day people were gaily trooping about the streets and into the stores, and there was no trouble from that time on. So peace came to one small city on Foothill Boulevard, and such as this you too can easily accomplish in prayer. The key to it is *expectancy*, seeing in the mind a peaceful town with freedom for all. You can do this—you really can—but the condition for bringing forth the peace of God in any such way is that you must *believe* it, and thereafter never again open your eyes to any other possibility, or open your mouth to talk of anything save the peace of God in that community.

This is the discipline of the prayer of faith, and it is truly a discipline!

One recent summer I visited a rancher and his family high in the mountains of Colorado. There amid snow-capped peaks lie deep valleys that are supposed to be covered with grass. But that year the usual rains had not fallen and the grass died, there being no arrangement for watering those broad acres. My host was considering bringing in grain to feed his cattle, but there was really no grain available, except at prohibitive prices. All spring the newspapers had apparently enjoyed prophesying that it would be a long hot summer and that famine would strike that part of the country.

So I instructed the family how to pray for rain, and then we prayed together, father, mother, and a number of the six children who were at home. I explained to the Lord that we really needed rain, and asked for it with great assurance. Then in the name of the Lord I talked to the jet stream. I don't know precisely what that is, but I am informed that it governs the weather—and God governs it, so no problem. I advised the jet stream in the name of the Lord to move over in whatever was the best way to cause rain in that part of the country. Then I spoke to the wind and said, "Now swing around and blow from the far sea, bringing a gentle rain to the thirsty fields." Finally, as an affirmation or statement of faith, we read together Psalm 65, the smaller children stumbling a bit over the words but all rejoicing in the rain that was to come.

That night as the family drove me to the airport the rain began. It rained for five days at that time; the drought was ended and there was no need to bring in grain for the cattle, perhaps somewhat to the disappointment of the gloomy journalists.

In that case it was easy to pray for rain because the rancher really loved his broad acres and it comforted his heart to see the Lord making them "soft with showers" (Ps. 65:10). In a different way I suppose that the farmer loved his cattle too, although he had their appointed end in sight.

As for wind, the Lord showed on a different occasion and in a somewhat embarrassing way how to pray for it to cease. I am not proud of it, but the Spirit says, "Speak!"

Several years ago I had a School of Pastoral Care that did not go well, chiefly because the location was poor. The schools have never gone as well since my husband died, and I have decided to retire from them, as from everything else that I do not want to do! A free weekend was before me, after which I had to go on another mission, and Edith and I took rooms at Tiburon, across the bay from San Francisco. I had caught a cold, no doubt due to my own ill humor, and so we stayed in that evening and amused ourselves by playing Patience. A great wind arose, and the big motel windows shook and rattled until we could hardly hear ourselves speak, and there seemed to be real danger of the glass blowing right in on top of us. It was all very annoying and suddenly, with no preconceived intention, I raised up a threatening hand and yelled at the wind at the top of my voice, "All right, that's enough! Quiet down!" It ceased blowing instantly. There was not another puff. In the morning the newspapers reported in dismay that for no ascertainable reason, the winds, which had been forecast to continue overnight at least, had abruptly ceased.

To this day I wonder about this perplexing incident! But apparently even through my ill humor I had discovered one of the laws of this kind of prayer for rain or sunshine, wind or calm. It is far more effective to talk directly to sea or sky, wind or storm, than simply to ask God to do this or that. We are God's agents upon this earth. When praying for people we ask in His name and by His power, because we so often lack the necessary understanding of the people for whom we pray. In praying for nature, however, it is more effective to speak directly to wind or storm or tempest. That, after all, is the way Jesus stilled the storm. "Peace, be still!" He cried, probably at the top of His voice that He might be heard above the wind's howling (Mark 4:39). And it ceased immediately.

We in His name are the overlords of this earth. We inherit the earth and it is up to us to subdue it. The earth knows us and responds to the command of faith.

Last spring there was a forest fire near my house, and the

wind was remorselessly pushing the brush fire closer and closer. One night I awoke after midnight and went out on my upper balcony where I could smell the smoke, and already knew from the papers that the winds were blowing it directly toward me. So I called aloud to the wind, muting my voice just a little bit lest I wake my neighbors: "Hear me, wind!" I said, holding out my hand in its general direction. "You are to swing around now and blow from the west, bringing in mist and rain from the sea. Come now! It may take you a little while to do so, but by morning let it be accomplished! Blow from the sea, and let the clouds gather and let a gentle mist or rain descend upon the burning areas and put out the fires. In the name of the Lord Jesus Christ I give you this order, and I rejoice, believing it will be so!"

And so it was. Wind, light, power—that energy from God is given to His children on earth to control in His name.

He is the Light. And when He said, "Let there be light," He dispatched, out of His own supply, light to whirl into our earth and sun and moon and universe of stars. God is light and is the source of light. And given to us is the great honor and obligation to understand both the light that is the light of God, and this earth upon which we have been placed, that we may order and direct it according to God's will. Jesus, the channel of the light to us, has told all this to us in many stories and parables, especially the one about the vineyard owner who asked his sons to go and work in his vineyard, and the husbandman who went on a far journey and commanded his servants to care for his fields and his pastures, nourishing and cherishing them until his return (Matt. 21:21-43).

Those who obeyed His commands would be received with rejoicing into the Father's house, while those who rejected them would be cast into outer darkness.

What is the Father's house? It is heaven and the heaven of heavens! And where is it? Floating around like a dream in space? Or on some far planet, or many far planets?—for more than one heaven is spoken of in the Bible. I am quite sure that there are many heavens, and the glory of one is not like the glory of another, and we go from glory to glory as we take care of this little earth upon which we now live.

CHAPTER 2

What if we do intend to enter into this venture in prayer for the earth, the vineyard our Father has given us to tend, but upon our first attempts at prayer, nothing happens. What do we do then?

First of all, we look to our connection; are our channels open to God? How much space are we giving Him that His light shall shine through us? Only a supernatural power can influence wind and tide, fire and flood. We cannot do it by ourselves. We can only build more stately mansions of the soul that His Spirit may occupy them and work through them.

> Build thee more stately mansions, O my soul
> > As the swift seasons roll!
> > Leave thy low-vaulted past!
> Let each new temple, nobler than the last,
> Shut thee from heaven with a dome more vast,
> > Till thou at length art free,
> Leaving thine outgrown shell by life's unresting sea.
> > > Oliver Wendell Holmes,
> *The Autocrat of the Breakfast Table*, ch. 4, "The Chambered Nautilus."

Or to use a different metaphor, let the measure and span of our light increase until it can encompass skies and seas and fire and tempest! Actually this is not a metaphor nor a simile. We are not now imagining ourselves a chambered nautilus growing a new shell. This is literal and true! We can acquire a current of spiritual energy so powerful that it can still tempests and put out fires, and cause rain to fall on parched land. The light-energy that is in us can merge with the light-energy of God through Jesus Christ and can accomplish these things. I could quote scores of Bible verses that say this, but I would rather suggest ways in which you can find it out for yourselves.

Before we undertake to pray for such great matters as the land and the waters, we should learn the ways of faith through praying about smaller matters. For instance, from time to time we are apt to have a concern for someone who is ill. We remember that James said, "The prayer of faith shall save the sick" (5:15). How do we go about praying that prayer of faith?

First, since God is love and His power moves only on the thought-waves of loving kindness, we can enlarge our channels by enlarging and expanding our loving concern for people, and our gentleness and kindness toward them. Strangely, it is just in this area that many truly devoted Christians fail to make the grade. Sometimes our very zeal is a barrier to us, leading us to be critical of others instead of having loving concern for them. Thus we cut ourselves off from the divine energy that produces the power, for instance, to quiet a city by prayer.

So let us search ourselves, not with dull remorse but with the excitement of searching for hidden riches. For that is exactly what we are doing. And if it is a nuisance to be kind to a bothersome neighbor, it is well worth it, for we are indeed searching for the buried treasure of divine power hidden within us.

It is hardly necessary to say: if we owe anything to anybody, pay it. If we have lied to anyone, confess the truth. If we are slothful in business, repent and ask God to teach us diligence. If we keep a sloppy house, clean it up and beautify it as unto the Lord. In fact, it would do no harm to read over the Ten Commandments much as we would check our appearance in a mirror before leaving the house.

But this is really difficult, you may be thinking. Naturally! God told us to overcome the earth and subdue it, but He never told us that it is an easy thing to do.

If we need more grace to accomplish this, there is no better place to find it than in our morning communion with God, our private prayer time. People have often asked me how I meditate and pray, and I have hesitated to tell them, but if we are going to do the greater miracles for which creation waits, we will need all the power available, so I will try to describe the indescribable.

The first necessity is to be regular in this time of communion with God; and I mean not so much regular according to the clock, for your time of rising may differ, but regular according to your schedule. I find that the best time is on first arising. Mothers with little children may have to attend to the children first and send them off to school, or if they are too young, get them fed and clothed and comfortable, so that they can be left for a while. Others can have this dynamic quiet time simply by setting the alarm clock a bit earlier. This is not a time for relaxing and letting the mind drift, but a time for renewing our hold on the current of spiritual energy which comes from God through Jesus Christ and His Holy Spirit, and is available to us.

It is glorious to have a special place for prayer, though I realize that not all people can at every stage of life have such a holy place of their own. If not, I hope that at least you can use the same place every morning, and that the time will come when you can have a prayer-room or study, and beautify it with growing things and inspiring pictures. This room of mine is on the lower floor of my split-level house, and I come downstairs in the morning with coffee to stay myself, and see again with a thrill of new delight my orchids that fill the corners of the room and the outdoor patio, hung over with bottle-brush and oleander. Yes, I know it sounds luxurious, but my little study in New England was even more exciting when bright geraniums and tender ferns shone on my window sills against a background of snow! Even my unpainted shack at my New England summer home became so full of the light of the Lord that my tiny grandson said on entering it, *"Who is in here?"*

As you can see, I love beauty. I think Jesus did too, and was cheered by the wild anemones (the "lilies of the field") and little ferns when He climbed a mountain to get away from man for a bit to glorify God and enjoy Him.

I sit comfortably, pray for my own protection, fold my hands, and lift up my spirit unto the Lord. There is nothing difficult about this. I just wait until I feel His presence. Then first of all, being a normal mother and grandmother, I name each of my children and grandchildren, praying for their protection as I have prayed for my own. "I sign _____ with the sign of the cross; I cover him with the blood of the Lamb; I surround him with the light of the cross; and in the name of Jesus Christ I say that nothing shall come through to hurt him." Sometimes I imagine God's light surrounding one or another of them with an actual aura or halo of an invisible energy of light, and I know that this is not fanciful, but true. God's light can so surround us.

After praying thus I sign Southern California with the sign of the cross, remembering that the Lord sent me here to pray for the protection of this land from destructive earthquakes. And I "see" this area brooded over by an invisible light that shines even into the troubled parts of the earth and helps them to settle their differences slowly, gradually, with no great upsets or loss of life. Earthquakes are not in themselves evil occurrences! A quake is simply caused by the growing process of land being gently heaved up out of the ocean through natural creation. It is the birth of new land and like childbirth, which is not evil either, it may need help. It may well be that man's interference with nature by exploding atomic bombs over and beneath the earth is increasing its disturbance. If so, it needs all the more help.

It pleases me thus to pray for the land; it brings deep comfort to my soul. And even though no one can predict to what extent this kind of prayer will really ease the evolvement of the earth, I know by my feelings, by the testimony of my spirit, that it is good.

Having thus prayed, I let my spirit free to see what else the Lord desires to tell me or to show me. Sometimes at this point I pray in the spirit rather than in English. And sometimes a voice seems to say within me, "Come on up," and I let my mind drift whither it would drift. I seem to see flower-filled meadows that are not of this earth, high mountains glimmering with a light whiter than snow, far places not upon this planet earth. It is as though one looks across the sea of life and sees the new country ahead. (This is one of the advantages of becoming old. In my younger days such glimpses of ultimate reality never came to me.)

Naturally my nerves are relaxed and at peace. I am not using them at the moment and they may rest. Therefore my spiritual energy is increased so that I feel I could move mountains—though I have not tried that as yet! I feel a part of this creation that waits for the manifestation of the sons of God, the children of God. Here I am. I am one with God's Spirit in me, and God's Spirit is in parched wheat fields and unsteady mountains and furious winds. Therefore I can pray for them not as a stranger but as one of those for whom the creation waits, one of the children of God.

It is for such as this, things greater than individual healings, that I am usually now called to pray. I wait every morning for the

Lord's guidance. He is able to veer my mind from here to there, to bring to my attention places far and near that need the prayer of faith for the healing of famine conditions, or the quieting of angry mobs, or the prevention or mitigation of earthquakes. I do occasionally pray for individuals also, when my family duties in prayer are over, but I do not keep a "list." People sometimes write and ask me to put their names on my list. I have no list. Sometimes I answer those letters, especially if a stamped envelope is enclosed, briefly saying that I send a prayer along with the letter. But I have no group of any kind at all, and this praying for individuals is no longer required of me by the Lord. He has turned my heart to other things.

The newspapers are a help to me, for they usually report parched fields that need prayer, or riotous conditions that can be quieted by prayer. If only every professing Christian would read the papers with the intention of praying for at least one of the threatening conditions reported therein, we would have a better world. In praying for such a condition as drought or famine, I remember the Lord's prayer, "Thy kingdom come, thy will be done on earth as it is in heaven." Would He will famine and starvation in heaven? Certainly not. Then certainly He does not will them on earth. So I take a particular place for my prayer-objective and help Him in prayer to supply its needs.

"Jesus can do everything!" some people say insouciantly, and dismiss the matter from their minds. It does not get done. Why? Truly, He can do everything if we, by becoming His helpers in prayer, fulfill the purpose for which He called us. We are, you might say, to be His partners. If we think of Jesus as merely a glorified Man stalking through the heavens, this does not make sense. He is more than that. He is the main conductor of the light, the creative energy of God into this world, and as such He needs helpers; He needs channels. A tree cannot bring forth fruit without the branches, any more than the branches can survive without the tree. We are the branches, or to return to

24

the previous analogy, we are the light bulbs through which God's light shines upon this earth. It is our duty to turn on this light by the prayer of faith. When we pray for a certain area of our earth, our light—God's light through us—actually reaches and penetrates that area. This sounds impossible, but here is one way of testing it if you like. Focus your eyes on a cloud in the sky and in silence, within your mind, tell that cloud to go away, to dissolve, to disappear. You had better make it a very small cloud, and not tell anyone what you are doing. This is just a sort of holy game, to increase your faith a bit. Then imagine the cloud melting as you look upon it, getting thinner and thinner, until it can be seen no more. If you have a mind like a little child, and can use your power of seeing by faith rather than your reasoning ability, the cloud will disappear. God's light has entered into it through you. In this small matter, He has permitted you to be a light-bearer—perhaps to show you that His light is real.

God is light. Jesus is the light-bearer. He is the light that lightens everyone upon this earth. We are to be His servants, His channels conducting by the prayer of faith His light to those parts of the earth that need it. Not too many, and not all at once! Remember, each of us is only one light bulb or channel. But if all of us who call ourselves Christians would read the newspaper in a spirit of prayer to see where to focus our light of faith, famines could be averted and uprisings quieted, and eventually when enough of us engage in this creative praying, wars will cease.

How sad and strange that most Christians utterly ignore their power and their duty to channel God's light to this world! When they read of an expected year of hunger, for instance, all they can think of is to raise money and ship grain here and there. How cumbersome and ridiculous, when we have the power to turn upon the afflicted country a current of God's healing light, *believing* that productivity will be increased and suffering averted.

This interrelation between God, His creation, and ourselves is not as strange as it might seem. God's light is the foundation of the being of all created things, conscious or unconscious. The Bible tells us this very clearly. "In the beginning God created the heaven and the earth" (Gen. 1:1). What material did He use in bringing forth the heaven and the earth and all the infinite family of stars? He used His own light, the light that is the light of men, the light that shineth in darkness unto this day. He used the energy of His own being, which is light shining with a greater intensity than any light that we can see or imagine. That was the basic material of all stars and planets, and of the infinite variety of things that grow and move upon them. So, God's light is in the fields and the forests, the mountains and the rivers and the sea.

Sometimes I feel sadness from the land upon my departure from a place I have loved. I am sure some of my readers have felt the same; I do not think we are imagining these things. I believe there can be an emanation of God's light in the very soil that in some dim way responds to our human feelings.

Most of all I feel God's light in the sea, that cradle of life that still gives life to those who look to it 'n love. Water seems to be a very powerful conductor of God's life. Is that not why water is always used in the sacrament of baptism?

When Jesus spoke to the sea and told it to quiet down, it obeyed Him. If He is the vine and we are the branches, if He is the powerhouse conveying God's power to us and we are the light bulbs getting our life from Him, then the sea should obey us also. Jesus spoke to the angry waves in order to save the life of His little boat and those therein. He would not have strolled beside the sea of Galilee and commanded it to be still just to amuse himself. But when men's lives or comfort needed it, then He did command the sea and it obeyed Him.

A member of a ship's crew who had learned prayer from me during an ocean voyage wrote me later that there had been a very rough day, much to the discomfort of the passengers. He

26

had wondered whether to tell the ocean to be still, as Jesus did, and he did try it; the wind died down immediately, the waves were stilled, and the passengers arose from their berths and disported themselves on deck.

But can I prove all this? No, I can't prove it. *You* can prove it for yourself. Try it and see!

Occasionally in our still valley of coastal California a sudden wind arises and roars down the canyon to the danger of my orchids and to the distress of many people, for trees can fall in winds like these, and even buildings can suffer damage. One night such a wind arose and I went out on my upper balcony and called out to it and said, "That's enough! Quiet down!" Immediately the wind ceased. That wind recognized the voice of God, its creator, that was in my small being, and obeyed.

Surely this is what God meant when He created the garden of Eden and then from the earth itself brought forth a man and a woman, and told them to dress it and to keep it.

In Genesis 1:28 God instructed man to replenish the earth, and subdue it. What if we try thus to "subdue" wind or fire, and nothing happens? What shall we do then? We had better try again to "build us more stately mansions," that is, to expand our spiritual beings. And so I suggest another way of doing this, which is to increase our knowledge and understanding of this world in which God has ordered us to work as His agents, and in so doing to expand our understanding of God.

God is a creator. The way that we appreciate any creator is by his works. How do we know that a man is a good musician? By hearing him play the piano or the violin, or whatever it is that he plays. How can we know that a person is a good artist? By looking at the pictures that he paints. How do we know that someone is a good doctor? By observing the efficacy of his cures. How do we know that God is a good creator? By understanding and appreciating His creation.

In our childhood, and in the childhood of the race, the

creation was considered to be the earth, with the sun to shine upon it by day and the moon to shine upon it by night, and the stars to add a bit of interest to the dark hours. This is very far from the truth. Actually, the earth is but one of several planets that rotate around the sun, and the moon is a small satellite rotating around the earth. Everything in the heavens moves; there is no such thing as a fixed body.

The sun is a raging, boiling vortex of unbelievable heat, beside which any fire would seem cool. And the stars are other suns, so far away from this solar system that distance is measured not in miles but in light-years. A light-year is the distance that light, at 186,000 miles per second, can travel in one year. I read in a book on astronomy that if a person lived on a planet rotating around even one of the nearer suns ("stars") and could see with a high-powered telescope all the way to this earth, he would be able to see Adam and Eve in the garden of Eden.

However, even the most high-powered telescope cannot see as far as any planet around any sun save ours. Astronomers can only deduce that, since our sun in earlier aeons threw off flaming matter that whirled into earths and moons, so, in all probability, the far stars would also have their satellites of earth or earths, and moon or moons.

Now consider this: Would the Creator in His tremendous passion for creation bring forth sentient life only on this planet? As we think of these things, we must of necessity also consider how God caused life to be upon this earth, life that culminated in human beings who, to some extent anyway, were to take over His control of the earth.

God made man of the dust of the earth. The very earth itself brought forth grass and trees and flowers, the fecundity of God bursting into active life, fed by His soil that He created, watered by His rains and warmed by His sun. How were grass and trees and flowers caused to live upon the earth? It would be

28

interesting to study geology, the science of the earth, and learn as much as we can about this, and yet we do not really need to do so, for we can just believe what the Bible says, that the Lord caused it to be. And this vegetation changed and increased as the principle of growth that God incorporated in the earth did its work. The Lord caused it to be so that instead of the primary vegetation of ferns and grass we now have added to that an immense number of fascinating trees and flowers. That is the way that God creates.

In a more mysterious and exciting way God caused this principle of life that is in the dust of the earth to bring forth, under His orders, fish in the sea and creeping things, and then animals upon the earth, and then man. So God made man out of the dust of the earth, and breathed into him the breath of life.

God's breath is God's Spirit, and His Holy Spirit coming upon Adam in whatever primal state of creation we do not know brought forth upon the earth beings capable of knowing their Creator.

One cannot help wondering at this point whether God created men or any kind of spiritual beings on any of the other earths in this vast universe. Apparently, in so far as astronomers can understand it, there are no human beings on any of the sister planets that rotate around our earth. Jupiter apparently cannot support life. Venus is surrounded by a cloud, fifty miles deep, and whether it is of steam or some other gases we do not know. It would seem unlikely that human life could have sprung up under these circumstances. Mars apparently has no water, and therefore could hardly support human life, though scientists are now endeavoring to ascertain whether there may possibly be the microscopic beginnings of life in the soil of Mars. Neptune and Uranus are too far away for anything except speculation.

Even a bit of an understanding of the creative laws through which God works helps us to believe in His power of re-creation. In the beginning God said, "Let there be light," and there was light, and that light is the life of man. That light is God's own creative energy, a tiny bit of the vibration of His own being, still operative in this world in two ways. The first way, as everyone knows, is the natural urge toward life that fills this earth in the most amazing ways. Tiny desert flowers manage to live in the strength of one rain a year, or less, plus the life of God constantly breathed into them. Little trees on high hills grow through rocks, actually splitting them in order to continue the struggle toward life. Plants may even come up through solid concrete, as an ambitious bamboo is doing in my own driveway. What is this passion for life, this terrific thrust toward bringing forth new life? This is God, forever creating!

Secondly, the same breath of God's life that urges plants to grow and flowers to bloom abides in us. It is the same light, the same flow of energy, and therefore we can in a mysterious way communicate with the world of nature. Even plants respond to love, and all love is of God. We read articles about this nowadays; the gardener plants two boxes of seeds, both alike, and speaks to one of love and light, while cursing and saying ugly words to the other. The first box of seedlings grows luxuriantly, and the other withers and dies. I have never needed the humiliation of doing this. (Wouldn't you feel queer if a neighbor came in and found you snarling over a box of seeds?) I *know* that it is so, for my love of flowers is an active love. When people say how wonderfully my roses grow, I know that it is not merely because I feed and water them regularly, but also because every day I walk among them and admire and love them. And they love me! The same creative light of God that is in them shines forth to love and to cherish me.

Do you know Sidney Lanier's poem, "A Ballad of Trees and the Master?"

Into the woods my Master went,
Clean forspent, forspent.

Into the woods my Master came,
Forspent with love and shame.
But the olives they were not blind to him,
The little grey leaves were kind to him,
The thorn-tree had a mind to him,
When into the woods He went.

Out of the woods my Master went,
And He was well content.
Out of the woods my Master came,
Content with death and shame.
When Death and Shame would woo him last,
'Twas on a tree they slew him—last,
From under the trees they drew him last:
When out of the woods he came.

There was a poet who grasped the reality of the life flow, from man to nature, from nature to man.

Once in England I met a retired army chaplain, who had been in campaigns all over the world and seen terrible things. He was a rough and grizzled personality, and in retirement his roses were his greatest interest. He told me, "When I prune my roses I talk to them, and explain that the prunings is for their own good, and they will feel much better. I pray for them too, and I ask them to pray for me." I myself have never gone that far, but how delightful to meet someone who has!

Can you imagine the flow of life, the very breath of God which is also a flow of love, permeating this earth and being the very ground from which miracles flow, the substance from which miracles are made?

Let us carry this thought a little bit farther. Is it ever the will of a gardener that one of his cherished plants should become riddled with blight or disease and wither and die? I think not! When a plant is too old to function properly, then he will probably cut it down and take its seeds to scatter on the ground and bring forth new plants. In the same way, when we are too old to function properly or to enjoy Him on earth, then God will permit the spirit to leave this body, and this body may die while the spirit goes on to a new kind of life in one of the heavenly places that He has prepared for us, one of the many "mansions" in His Father's house (John 14:2). There is no mention in the Bible of any human being ever being re-born on this earth, and in that dismal theory of reincarnation I do not at all believe, praise God! But in eternal life I do believe, for it is the promise of the scriptures and the very purpose for which Jesus came into the world.

Since in due time this body must be prepared to "give up the ghost" (spirit) that herein dwells, I would hesitate to pray for a very old person to get well on this earth, unless there seemed to be a very good reason for it. I prefer to pray for that person to be comforted and upheld for as long as he or she is destined to be on this earth, and then to have a happy entrance, a happy landing, as it were, in God's heavenly kingdom.

Why do so many of us, Christians as well as unbelievers, suffer illnesses that are not always healed by prayer? And why do some people fail to live up to the laws of the Lord, even when they have accepted Him as their Lord and Savior? And why does calamity sometimes befall not only the unjust but also the "just"?

You have guessed it. There is a contrary force upon our planet, which we call Satan or the devil, for so he is named in the Bible. He fell upon this earth in the very beginning. "I beheld Satan as lightning fall from heaven," said Jesus (Luke 10:18), and he tempted the newborn inhabitants of the garden of Eden to disobey the commands of God and to eat (absorb into their being) the fruit, or result, of knowing not only good but also evil (Gen. 3).

I am translating the Old Testament story into words that make more sense to me, but if you prefer to think that Adam "ate" the apple, as people say (though the word "apple" is not found in

Genesis), then follow your own understanding of that sad passage. At any rate, the first people on earth disobeyed God, and thus left a door open for Satan to come to them. Satan is a spiritual being, not physical, but he is evil. According to the Bible he was meant to be good, he was created good, but he disobeyed God and could therefore no longer abide in heaven and so found a landing place on this new planet, earth. Does this sound like a fairy tale? Perhaps when we get to heaven we will find that it is no fairy story, and perhaps long before we reach our heavenly home we will know that it is true, that there *is* a tempter who tries to separate us from God.

One of his favorite ways of doing so is to sneak into our bodies, or rather, to project his evil into our bodies and thus cause illness. This in no way means that only evil people become ill. Quite the contrary. It is more to the benefit of the devil to project an illness into a good person than into a bad one. I am not speaking here of the demonic possession that is sometimes evident in mental illness, but of the ordinary bodily illnesses to which mankind is subject. And I do not mean that Satan is personally responsible for all illnesses. I only mean that the air around is filled not only with the radiance of God through Jesus Christ, but also with dark shadows which have polluted the very air. In that darkness we are without the protection of the light of Christ, and so illness is apt to come upon us. To a considerable extent we can avoid it and remain healthy if we daily renew our connection with the Lord, and so are filled anew with His light. Thus we can be clothed with light like heavenly armor, but let there be any crack in our armor and the old enemy is apt to sneak in.

Cracks in our spiritual armor are not limited to outward sins. They, of course, do expose us to the machinations of the enemy, but there are other ways in which we can become exposed. One of them is the mistake of thinking that every kind of meditation is of God. In some kinds of meditation, unfortunately very popular in our day, the conscious mind is shut off as much as possible, letting the unconscious drift free without anchor or guide. This may induce temporary feelings of joy and mystic bliss, but it exposes the "heart," as the Bible calls the unconscious mind, to the power of the enemy. "Keep thy heart with all diligence; for out of it are the issues of life" (Prov. 4:23). We need constantly to protect the inner mind by the name of Jesus. His name is indeed our shield, as we read in the Bible and sing in the old hymns. Therefore, I have learned through long experience that Christians run into danger when they expose their hearts to the enemy by taking part in any form of meditation that is not Christ-centered. It opens a door to the enemy, and it can be a cause of illness. So can sin, of course, living in anger and resentment instead of in the love of Christ, living in a dishonorable relationship instead of in the purity demanded by God, in fact living contrary to any of the Ten Commandments in which God laid down the laws of life. These commandments are not arbitrary rules made by a capricious prophet. Rather, they are God's original, inbuilt laws, and they open the doors of our souls to His light. He that does not keep them walks in darkness, and in that darkness the enemy can find him, trouble him, or even in the end destroy him.

So, to make it all very simple, it may possibly be that our prayers for the healing of ourselves or of another are held up by some sin. The light cannot break through to us, or through us to others. "If therefore the light that is in thee be darkness, how great is that darkness!" (Matt. 6:23).

If our prayer of faith for someone who is ill does not bring an answer, what then shall we do? We should never say to a sick person, "What are you doing that is wrong?" because that is only likely to startle or infuriate him, and thus to shut the door even more tightly.

First, let us search our own souls, asking the Lord how to

open the doors of our own hearts more widely, and praying for Him to show us where we may be doing or thinking what displeases Him. Then, if we are quiet and listen, we may be guided to correct some injustice in our lives, or to forgive someone who does not like us, praying for that person with genuine love. While engaged in all this thought and prayer, we of course also speak strongly to the enemy, telling him that we are surrounded by the light of Christ, that we are cleansed by the blood of the Lamb, and that he cannot come near us or into us. Then, having cleared our hearts as best we can, we once more pray for the healing of the sick person, never, never saying to him that Satan must be in him preventing his healing. Heavens, we would scare him to death! No, if by chance Satan is in the sick person it is up to us who pray to take command in the name of Jesus Christ and (usually in silence) tell him to leave. If the person himself expresses a sense of Satan's interference, then we can agree aloud to tell Satan in the name of Jesus Christ to get away from him. We have perfect authority for this, and the enemy will obey that command given in the name of Jesus Christ. His darkness cannot remain in the face of that light. As I sometimes tell a troubled person, when we turn on the light in a room, the darkness *has* to go away. We don't need to say, "Go away, darkness!" for it simply cannot stand against that light. This is not the casting out of an evil spirit, known as exorcism. It is merely helping a sick person to remove any darkness of soul which may have opened a door to illness.

Sometimes we find out, or gather in conversation, that an illness is connected with memories of the past, such as the feeling of not being wanted as a child. In this case we can very simply ask Jesus to open the doors of the past and let His light shine all the way back to childhood, healing not only the person who is now ill but healing also the little child still living within all the darkness of feeling unwanted and unloved, letting God's light shine in all the way, through the memories of a lifetime.

This healing of the memories (a phrase given me directly by the Lord, many years ago) should always be surrounded by the love of Christ, and done in His gentleness and through His power of forgiveness. It should be done, moreover, by one person for one person, not in a group. I have sometimes, in later years, prayed in a general way for a whole congregation at once, but I am still sure that the most effective method of praying for the healing of the memories, because it is the most loving, the most gentle, and the most considerate, is one to one, as private as the confessional should be. This is the way Jesus worked. When He said to someone in deep trouble, "Thy sins be forgiven thee," He did not call upon a group of the disciples to join Him in that announcement. To do so would have been unnecessary, as well as confusing to the heart, the deep mind. Jesus is Lord of love, not of confusion.

Having stated my conviction that prayer for the healing of the memories is best done individually and privately, I do want to tell the story of a lovely experience when I did it the other way, praying for the Lord to heal the memories of a whole group at once. It was at one of my last Schools of Pastoral Care, with about seventy-five people, mostly clergy, present. We had been together thinking on the things of the Lord for five days, sharing deep fellowship in the Spirit, and I believe that is why the prayer was so effective.

A Catholic monk, a missionary on furlough from South America, told me this story of his experience while I was praying. As I asked them all to do, he let his mind wander back over his lifetime and came to himself at the age of about eight, an unhappy, lonely child. Jesus came to him in a sort of vision, I suppose, and asked him if he were all right, and happy. The little boy said no, he was all alone, and sad.

"Oh, I'll go and get my mother," said Jesus, and He went away and soon came back with His mother, Mary. He left the two of them together, and Mary took the lad in her lap and held him close, and comforted him.

After a while she said, "Are you happy now?"

"Yes," said the little boy, "but I'm still lonely. I haven't anybody to play with."

"Oh," said Mary, "I'll go and get my little boy."

She disappeared and soon returned with the boy Jesus, also about seven or eight years old. He was dressed, the priest told me, in a rather sissy costume of white robe and sash, like a Bedouin, with a turban on His head. The two children stood and looked at each other; Mary was there no more.

"What do you like to do?" asked the child Jesus of the vision.

"I like to skip stones in the brook," said the boy who later became a priest.

So they went down to the brook and skipped stones and played in the water, getting their shoes and all their clothes rather wet. They took off their shoes, and thought it would be fun to exchange them, and then went on to exchange clothes as well, Jesus putting on the little American boy's sailor suit, and he the Lord's white robe. Thus it came to pass that in the vision Jesus stood on the earth in the shoes of a man, and the little boy was clothed in the white robes of righteousness.

Though the little boys did not see them, I am sure the angels were there beholding and wondering. The priest told me with overflowing joy that he was healed during that prayer of a whole lifetime of loneliness and depression.

We can do well to study how Jesus carried on His ministry among sick and troubled people. He never said, "Do you want me to forgive you?" nor, "Tell me more. What else have you done that is wrong?" His was the gentle and perfect way of love—but not because He was a sissy! When He made a scourge of small cords and threw out those who were defiling the temple of His Father, he was no sissy! He was more like a roaring lion, but if any of those moneychangers had come to ask for His forgiveness, then He would not have roared but would have shown the utmost tenderness, as He did to the thief on the cross.

CHAPTER 3

God's Holy Spirit, God's light, they are the one life-energy of God shining eternally from Him in varying ways. Today we hear a good deal about receiving the Holy Spirit, and that is good, but I believe that we receive Him, the Light-giver, in more than one way. The first way is in the rite of baptism. In churches practicing infant baptism, the priest or minister prays that the soul of the infant may be set free from sin—not its own, of course, for how could a tiny baby have sinned? No, the sins of the forefathers have made an inherited bondage, a built-in tendency toward darkness. Some call this Satan, though that seems to me in this case a somewhat too lurid description, but in a sense it is true, for surely this darkness, these inborn tendencies to lie and steal and hurt, do not in the first place come from God. Could it not be said that baptism would bring such light of God into the infant's newborn, groping mind that it is a first step toward the illumination of the Holy Spirit?

Once I walked down a New England hill with one of my grandchildren, who was about four years old. "Who is God?" he asked. I tried to explain that God is like a great big shining light that is so bright that we cannot see Him.

"But I can," said the little boy serenely. I have no doubt whatsoever that he could, and did, and believe that he received that spiritual gift of seeing God through baptism. I do not believe that this ability to see and know God is inborn in everybody. The Chinese children among whom I was brought up, quaint and loveable as they were, certainly did not see God's light, and as soon as they were old enough to understand anything they were apt to learn from their elders, quite tragically, to "see" demons and devils. They were terrified of them.

After baptism many of us receive the rite of confirmation or, in other communions, join the church, becoming part of the Christian fellowship. This is a tremendous opportunity for the entering in of a new and powerful current of God's light, but in many cases the door of the soul of those confirmed or received into church membership is not open to the fullness of the Holy Spirit. Understanding is not expected of an infant being baptized, but understanding is expected of those on the verge of maturity, so that a wider channel may be opened in their minds for the Holy Spirit to enter in and *illumine* and *enlighten* them. These are old words, all about the light of God. I know of churches in which the ministers have received a real illumination of the Holy Spirit, including all the gifts listed by Paul in 1 Corinthians 12, not only wisdom and knowledge, but also the vocal gifts, prophecy, tongues, and interpretation. One such minister requires the young people considering confirmation to attend a class weekly for six months. At one recent confirmation service, many of the confirmed people spoke in other tongues at the altar rail, scaring the visiting bishop nearly to death!

Most of us, however, are not so fortunate as to have such a minister or priest. How then can we receive the promises of Jesus? "And I will pray the Father, and he shall give you another Comforter, that he may abide with you for ever; even the Spirit of truth; whom the world cannot receive, because it seeth him not, neither knoweth him: but ye know him; for he dwelleth with you, and shall be in you" (John 14:16-17).

How shall we receive this Spirit of life and light? I have had three quite different experiences of receiving the light and the Light-giver; every time I have opened the door by asking for it, even though at first I did not know what I was asking.

The first occasion was long ago when I was still hauling myself with God's help out of a state of mental depression. My husband and I were in a little rented cottage by the lake in Alstead, New Hampshire. We had a housekeeper to live in the rectory in New Jersey and take care of the children, and we went off on a little vacation by ourselves. One bright, cold October morning I rowed across the lake, dragged the boat up on a pebbly beach, and climbed out of it. I lay down on the pine needles beneath some trees and sunbathed. Lying there entirely alone, for the lake was deserted in the fall, I prayed that God's light would come into me through the sun. I imagined that light entering into the whole of my being, and so it did. The experience was unlike anything that ever happened to me before or since. I *felt* the light, like an intense heat shining into me, and I was filled with a sudden bliss that was so great I could hardly stand it. It was frightening, yet I didn't want it to stop. But stop it did, just as I was crying out in my mind, "Lord, if this doesn't stop soon, I'll die!"

It ceased, leaving me shaken to the depths. For days my head felt tight, as if there were a band around it, a pressure which made me begin to wonder if I were developing a brain tumor. But it gradually went away, and the peace of the Lord, which seemed to be the aftermath of the light, remained with me.

I now understand that feeling of pressure. Something really was changing or enlarging within my head. This understanding came to me during the second experience of receiving the Holy Spirit which was at the home of a friend in Tucson, Arizona. I have spoken and written of this experience before, but I will briefly repeat it. My hostess, another woman, and I had decided that we needed the gift of the Holy Spirit, for all of us were worn out with praying for other people. As we meditated on this the Lord sent us an angel, as I always say when telling this story. He was a medical doctor who had heard of my visit and came to see us because of his interest in the things of the Spirit. His concepts and knowledge were different from ours. His specialty, he said, was the study of the inside of the head, where he found glands which should have been rounded out but which were flattened like balloons which had lost most of their air. He perceived also what he believed to be the shrunken remains of channels connecting these glands. He said he had always wondered whether it might be possible for a person to receive such a charge of spiritual energy that these glands (which he considered to be connected with man's spiritual perception) would come back to their normal shape and size, and the channel between them would be restored, thus reviving man's natural spiritual heritage.

We had no idea whether what the doctor said was scientifically sound, and that did not really matter. At least his words filled us with a great sense of expectancy, and the three of us continued in prayer with an enlarged concept of what might happen. I have often told of the great glory that burst upon us, though without any other physical signs except a deep burning and sense of pressure within the head. I have also told of the joy and peace of the Lord that filled us all, and how our symptoms of weariness and strain were totally and immediately healed. The gift of tongues did not accompany this experience, and I rejoice that it did not, for if we had spoken in tongues then we might have missed the deeper and more important healings of the inner being which took place in us all.

My third great experience of the Holy Spirit was on another occasion when I was again in Tucson visiting the same friends, who had by this time received the gift of tongues. They had written me about it, much to my dismay, because I felt that such a thing was definitely beyond the teaching of the Southern Presbyterian Church, in which I had been brought up. However, when we met in prayer, the three of us and two young men at home from college, I heard them speaking quietly in tongues. To me it sounded quite rational, though not understandable, rather as if I were listening to Chinese speaking in dialects that I did not know.

My initial reluctance even to think about speaking in tongues left me instantly, and when they laid hands on me and prayed I also received this gift, and from that day on have been able to use it at will. It has added to the joy of the Lord, and I have found it a quick and sure way of releasing in my being the Spirit of God, opening the way to the more important gifts of wisdom, knowledge and discernment. Therefore it helps in healing. However, if I were to compare these three adult experiences, this last one would be the least important. The most wonderful was certainly the receiving of God's light through the sun; I have never forgotten the tingling bliss of that rush of spiritual energy. Second would be the receiving of the Spirit through prayer with my two friends, and its awakening within me of what I call the primary spiritual gifts, those promised by Jesus himself in His final discourse to His disciples (John 14-17): the gift of joy; the gift of peace that comes from a more usable synchronization of mind and subconscious mind, of "heart" and body; and the gift of the understanding of truth. These became obvious to me not by any sensations at the moment, but as the days passed I perceived that my mind and my body worked together with much more ease and efficiency.

All these experiences opened in me more and more doors to the light of God. How then shall I keep them open? By using the light, not only for my own joy but for bringing forth light and healing in the earth as well as in other people. This light is not given to us merely to be frittered away in getting together with a few friends, for instance, and speaking in tongues. I consider that a waste of God's time, when the earth is struggling in darkness. Nor is the Spirit of the Lord satisfied if we limit ourselves to passing on the light to others. That is like trying to prepare a garden by equipping more and more people with spades. The spades alone do no good! They are meant to be used, and if we stand around with our spades in our hands, and praise the Lord continually for the glorious gift of spades while the garden is filled with weeds, the Lord of the garden of this earth is apt to be out of patience with us. He has in fact told parables about this very thing (Luke 20:9-16). The Lord of a vineyard went away on a long journey and commanded his servants to take care of the vineyard until his return. The servants neglected the vineyard, and fell to rioting and abusing each other instead, saying to themselves, in effect, "Oh, well, when the Lord of the vineyard returns, he will take care of everything." But the Lord of the vineyard returned and was wroth with those servants because they neglected his vineyard. He threw them out and hired others.

We are the stewards whom the Lord has left in charge of the vineyard of this earth. He is no longer here in the flesh to go across the lake in a little boat and still the waves when they become too boisterous. Nor, apparently, does He intend to personally direct the action of wind and waves at all times, any more than a vineyard owner plans to pick all the grapes himself, but has men working under him. God has men and women working under Him. Who are they? They are you! They are us!

I first learned this when I lived in New England. There were years when destructive hurricanes roared up out of the Gulf of Mexico along the New England coast, leaving havoc in their wake. These hurricanes would be predicted on the radio, with warnings repeatedly issued, hours in advance. At last a faithful prayer partner and I realized that we should do something about it. So when a hurricane was forecast we would pray for the power of the Lord to divert the storm and save the New England coast. Praying thus we spoke to the wind currents and told them in the name of Jesus Christ to avoid our coastline. They did! But we soon understood that our prayers were not going far enough because we were not instructing these hurricane winds where they should go. Once to our dismay a hurricane headed inland from our area and dumped its torrents of water into the Connecticut River valley, causing terrible devastation in cities there.

So the next time a hurricane was predicted with the likelihood that all inhabitants of the northeastern seaboard would have to be evacuated, we prayed for the Lord to divert the hurricane out to sea. Then, realizing the danger to shipping, we further prayed that it would quiet down and cause no danger to anyone. We spoke to the winds, even as Jesus did. Remember, "The works that I do shall he [who believes in Jesus] do also" (John 14:12). "Now, quiet down," we said, not in a reverent murmur but loudly, stretching forth our hands to the direction whence the hurricane was coming. "Quiet down! Blow out to sea now, gently, gently. Quiet down and blow out to sea!" And it did.

It is easier to do this kind of command-praying with two or three people than alone, but it does not work well in a more sizeable group. I have tried it, but there is apt to be someone who does not agree concerning it. One time in California I prayed for rain during a lecture on faith. A lady said to me afterwards, "I wish you wouldn't do that!"

"Why?" I asked in some surprise.

"Don't pray for rain! I've been praying for it not to rain ever since last fall, because my roof is in bad shape and I'm afraid it will leak."

I asked her why she didn't just get the roof repaired, but got no reply. When I prayed for rain at Melodyland, as I have already recounted, the prayer was answered promptly and in wonderful amounts, but there we had a deeply united, believing congregation who had agreed together concerning the need for rain.

Many questions come to mind at this point. First, why does not God simply control the weather himself, making it perfect according to His will at all times? It may be because He does not want us to continue forever being babes in the faith, fed out of His milk bottle, as it were. He wants us to grow up and learn to manage His estate, the earth, ourselves, with His aid behind us.

Another point comes to mind here. Why does it matter whether those in a group are in agreement or not? Can't God sort it out? Yes, of course, but He doesn't want to be forever sorting out our prayers. He wants us to learn, to take control, to have dominion. Moreover, prayer is not merely a matter of asking God. It is a matter of providing a channel through which God can do His will on this earth. We do ask, yes, but as we do God uses our spiritual energy, drawing the light out of us and sending it to the object of our prayers so that His will may be done.

But how do we know that we have any light that we may lend to God for His use? Would you like to know? Then look and you can see it; I will tell you how to see your own light, as a friend long ago told me.

Look toward a cloudy sky, and then withdraw your vision and focus on an area about three or four feet in front of your eyes. Do you see little specks of light dancing in the air? I saw them even as a child and thought they were the sunbeams. But they are not directly from the sun. They are an emanation of light from ourselves, our own spiritual light visible to us as little shining specks in the air around us.

Some people see this light in different ways, for instance as a halo around the head of someone filled with the light of Christ. I do not see this as easily as some people do, but at times I too have seen it around the head of a lecturer or preacher caught up in the joy of the Lord. It looks exactly like the halos depicted in

46

some of the ancient paintings of Jesus or His mother. That is not strange; the artists were simply painting what they saw.

So we really are the channels through whom God projects His light to the world. We do not know all that He does with this light, but to some extent we can see that He draws an energy from us ourselves, an energy produced by faith, through which He can answer the prayers of our hearts.

"There is always a light around Agnes's house," said a little boy once. "Kind of like a shiny cloud. Don't you see it?" No, I do not *see* God's protection around my house, but I absolutely know that it is there and that He cares for my little dwelling place just as He cares for all the loving, living things upon the whole earth. "But why should God care about the earth?" some people say. They believe that the Creator cares for us, His people, but somehow do not grasp the fact that He also has a concern for the earth itself.

Why not? I am a very imperfect reflection of a little of His image, and yet I care for this earth and especially for the garden that I have planted upon it. I go out on my upstairs verandah in the late afternoon and watch the shadows lengthen on the mountains while James, my pet wild bluejay, hops near and eats bits of crackers out of my hand. There I sit and look down at my orchids shining from the lower level of my garden dug out of the steep hillside, and delight in the oleander and red bottle-brush tree, and in the little canyon below, full of trees and bushes in every shade of green and silver. I look beyond to peaceful rooftops visible through the trees in soft shades of green and grey and gold, and beyond them I lift my eyes to the high mountains where the afternoon shadows are beginning to creep down into their canyons. I love it all! I appreciate it not only with the sight of my eyes but with a deep flow of love released within my heart, which may be lonely because I have been alone all day, or disturbed because too many people have been telling me their troubles. It comforts me to rest in the beauty of this garden that I have made.

Why should God not care about the earth itself, and be comforted by its beauty, and on the contrary be upset when people have not kept it beautiful? "They have made my pleasant portion a desolate wilderness," God said to Israel through His prophet Jeremiah (12:10).

How wonderful that we can give joy and comfort to our Lord by making beauty in the earth that He created! We are doing so. True, one can see a beer can beside the road. True, there are places where the natural beauty has been disturbed by highways which lead out to the glory of the wilderness, so that more people can enjoy its beauty. But on the whole this earth of ours is full of beauty, and it is our duty and our joy to see it and to enjoy it forever, as we are to enjoy the Lord our God forever.

An elderly lady was once heard to remark, "Isn't it lovely the way people are planting gardens and trees, making everything lovely for the return of our Lord!" It is lovely, and it is exactly the way the Bible tells us to prepare for the return of the Lord of the vineyard, the owner of the estate, the King of whole world!

Now I want to suggest a practical prayer project, a very thrilling one: choose a city and pray for the light of God to be increased in that city and for the peace of the Lord to brood over it. Pray that there may be no riots or burnings or strife, but that all may dwell together in increasing harmony and peace. Having chosen your city, pray thus for it every day, and make your prayer effective by believing that it will be answered—that it is being answered even while you pray. You can have great and holy fun with this prayer, imagining the Christian love that you will find in your city. Christian love does not have to be, and indeed cannot be, created by passing new laws. It does not need new laws, only new love.

For instance, I knew a lady in a southern city who was crippled from infancy with infantile paralysis. Her hands were not affected, and being a musician she supported herself by giving piano lessons. She lived in her old family home, but converted the upper floor into an apartment, which at one time needed repainting, so she called a painter who happened to be a black man. He came after church on Sunday looking very handsome in his blue suit. She explained what she wanted, and then started to go up the stairs, hauling herself painfully from step to step. "Miss Brown, you aren't going to walk up those steps," said the painter. "I'm going to carry you up."

So he picked her up in his arms, she put an arm around his shoulders, and he carried her upstairs and set her down in a chair while she explained the work she wanted done. Then he carried her downstairs again. "And when I get done with the painting," he said, "I'm going to carry you up again so you can see it. I don't want you walking up those stairs."

It so happens that the person from whom I learned my way of praying for peace in the cities is a black lady. I had met her first at a Camps Farthest Out meeting and knew her great power in prayer as well as preaching. One afternoon she led a prayer group in a somewhat unusual way. She asked each one of us to choose a city, and to keep our choice secret, since there is often more power in prayer when we do not tell anyone our objective. Then we went out on the grounds of the conference center, and stretched forth our hands toward the cities of our choice, praying for God's light to be projected into them and for these cities to be kept in peace. Then we imagined Jesus himself entering each city and saying, "Peace, be still!" and gave thanks believing that this would be so.

So far as I know we have kept our secret trysts with our cities to this day. In spite of newspaper prophecies that year that we would have "a long, hot summer," there was outward peace in the big cities of the North and Northeast, at least supplying the climate in which inner peace, the real peace of God, can grow and flourish in the hearts of His children.

What would happen in our world if every Christian would

undertake to pray the prayer of faith for one city, creating in our minds the picture of that city as a safe place, where people can walk at night without danger and can learn to live together as the children of God!

Why not try it? Imagine the light of God actually increasing in the city of your choice, so that all the products of that light—peace, prosperity, and the joy of the Lord—fill that city street by street, and neighborhood by neighborhood, so that even to drive through its streets gives strangers a sense of peace. They cannot see the light, but they would be able to feel it!

This would be like the millennium, you may say. Well! Let us by all means have a millennium, a thousand years of peace, and the sooner the better!

A young friend of mine found a rattlesnake in the family swimming pool when he was preparing for his morning dip. The snake was struggling about in the water, and did not seem happy there. The young man didn't know how it had gotten into the pool—perhaps it had fallen out of the overhanging trees—but there it was, out of place and unhappy. "I picked it up and stroked it a little," the lad told his mother later. "I sort of patted it and loved it, you know. It liked that. It didn't bite me. Then I took it down into the canyon and let it go."

There was a foretaste of the kingdom of heaven! "The sucking child shall play on the hole of the asp, and the weaned child shall put his hand on the cockatrice' den." So spoke the prophet Isaiah (11:8).

So we can help to build the foundation of the kingdom of heaven *now*, and the beginning of action for most of us is not rattlesnakes or mosquitoes (my nemesis!), either one, but people.

"People is more trouble than anybody in this world," said a wise youth in a country grocery store. "Last week they bought all my carrots, so this week I stocked up with a whole lot of carrots, and now they don't want any," and he repeated, "People is more trouble than anybody in this world."

So our Lord must have found it when He was down here among us. Nevertheless, people can be reached by prayer. A woman told me that she dreaded going to her office to work because everybody there was so mean and disagreeable. I told her to ask Jesus to go before, and fill that office with His light; then she should imagine that light shining into every person who worked in the office. In one week she came back and told me with amazement that the whole office had changed. Now it was full of the feeling of peace and joy that Jesus brings when His Holy Spirit fills a place, and she loved going there to work, as did the others. "They don't know what's happened in that office, but they *like* it!" she said.

On my last visit to Hawaii I had a mission in an Episcopal church, concluding with a healing service conducted by the minister, since I had retired from that kind of exhausting work some years before. So after my talk the minister seated me in a chair in the sanctuary, where I could see all that went on at the altar rail. Three men did the laying on of hands: the rector, his assistant, who was Japanese, and a visiting Methodist minister. The people came and knelt until they had been prayed for. In the very mixed congregation I saw a tall, rangy blond youth come and kneel, waiting his turn. It was the Japanese man, with shining blue-black hair who came to him. The long-haired tawny youth looked up at him and whispered something which of course I could not hear. Then the Japanese minister gathered him into his arms, as a mother might gather up her baby, and held him thus while he prayed for him.

The kingdom of heaven is not as far away as we might have thought!

CHAPTER 4

There are people who do not believe that the kingdom of heaven is very near to us, even though Jesus himself said to the disciples, "Lift up your eyes, and look on the fields; for they are white already to harvest" (John 4:35). Jesus warned His disciples however, telling them that a great tribulation awaited Jerusalem, and that a time of persecution must be endured by Christians before the kingdom of heaven would be finally established on the earth. The Great Tribulation came to Jerusalem about forty years after Jesus' ascension when the Roman armies laid the city waste, not leaving one stone upon another, even as Jesus had foretold. The time of persecution came a bit later, under the Roman emperor, Nero. It was those who held fast to their faith in spite of persecution, and died with the name of Jesus on their lips, who became the forerunners of our present churches.

Some Christian people today, however, not realizing that these prophesied events are past, still look for them in the future, and spend their time wondering when Jesus intends to come again. Come again He surely will, but He does not encourage us in these wonderings. When asked by His disciples about His

Second Coming, He replied, "But of that day and hour knoweth no man, no, not the angels of heaven, but my Father only" (Matt. 24:36).

Yet some people instead of working with all their heart and strength in building His kingdom on this earth, and praying for it with real belief as we are instructed to do in the Lord's prayer, are frittering away their time in trying to figure out *when* it will come, instead of tending this earth which is His vineyard. Maybe He will come in the year 2000, they say. The year 2000 is indeed the end of a millennium, the end of an age, and whether any significant changes will come to mark the new age I do not know.

But the end is not yet. Jesus said, "And ye shall hear of wars and rumours of wars: see that ye be not troubled" (Matt. 24:6).

The destruction of Jerusalem is past and gone, and Jesus has not returned save in our hearts. The time of persecution has for the most part passed. The time when soldiers would break into any house and haul away men and women and children who prayed in the name of Jesus, and throw them to the lions has *passed.* Even the echoes of it that still linger in China, Russia and other countries under dictatorship are diminishing, becoming less and less, and still Jesus has not yet returned in glory. We want Him to return, don't we? Then let us not make it more difficult for Him by dwelling on and looking for the very things that we *don't* want! Christians who in their ignorance look forward to persecution and distress are bringing trouble upon themselves, and it is only by the grace of God that we have come as far as we have. Instead of trying to figure the time of His final return, we would do better to concentrate on making this earth clean and beautiful for the Lord when He does return.

Suppose a mother said to her children, "I am going away for a while. I will return; I can't tell you exactly at what time, but while I am away I want you little children to pick up all your blocks and toys from the living-room floor. And you big boys, I would be

pleased if you would mow the lawn. And you two girls, will you
please wash the breakfast dishes and clean up the kitchen for
me?"

What if the children said among themselves, "Mother has
gone away, and we don't know when she will come back," and
neglected to pick up their toys, and let the lawn go untended,
and left all the dirty dishes in the kitchen, while they ran out to
play shouting gaily, "Mother's coming home after a while!" and
playing guessing games as to the exact time.

Mother would come home all right, and when she came there
would be trouble.

This is exactly what Jesus said in more than one parable. I
have already referred to the one beginning in Matthew 21:33,
and we would do well to read and study the others on the same
theme. A vineyard owner goes away, leaving his servants in
charge, and when he comes back and finds that they have
neglected his vineyard and spent their time in idling and
merrymaking, there is trouble. For whom? For his own servants!
He fires them all; he casts them out. There would be no use in
their saying, "But Master, we love you, and we were looking
forward to your return!" He would tell them to depart from him,
for they did not obey him.

Yes, the Lord is coming again, and in due time this planet
earth will in all probability be destroyed by fire. Nothing in the
universe is static, and nothing will remain forever except the
Creator of the universe, God, and His Son Jesus Christ. Even
the earth and the star that controls this earth and gives it life, the
sun, will cease. The heavens, the skies of our earth, will be rolled
up like a scroll and disappear, and the earth will be destroyed by
fervent heat (2 Pet. 3:10).

None of the stars, which are suns, remember, are destined to
shine forever. They may lose their light, or they may contract,
from having given out so much light, and explode. I envy
astronomers who know so much about events in outer space

because they can *see* them! With their high-powered telescopes they can make out amidst the bright shining of the heavens an occasional black star, a heavenly body remaining but no longer shining, having given out all its light. Then from time to time they have seen an explosion, a star of medium size suddenly bursting into great light, becoming a "nova" as it is called. (It is possible that the star of Bethlehem might have been a "nova" suddenly appearing in glory.)

"Wandering stars, to whom is reserved the blackness of darkness for ever." So wrote St. Jude (v. 13). There really are such stars in the sky, black stars, invisible yet perceptible to astronomers by the effect they have on other stars.

As I have already mentioned, the rational calculations of scientists suppose that our sun may explode in about fifty billion years, give or take a few. Many people couple the "end of the world" with the Second Coming of Christ. They mean the end of our solar system, and if the earth is tottering uneasily on its axis some fifty billion years from now, I can easily picture Jesus coming back here on a special rescue mission, snatching away those whose faith makes it possible, so that they will escape the final total destruction of this planet. What will He do with them, I wonder? "In my Father's house are many mansions," He said. ". . . I will come again and receive you unto myself" (John 14:2-3).

Where will all this be? In heaven, yes, but what is heaven? And what will we do there? From earliest childhood, the one daunting aspect of heaven for me was in the area of tedium! But as I come nearer to my time of departure to one of those heavenly "mansions," I do not believe that life there will be tedious. "His servants shall serve him," in eternity as well as on this earth (Rev. 22:3). How shall we serve Him? At this point I am going to tell you of the most wonderful and exciting dream I ever had.

I was on another planet, seemingly a very new planet, for it had no trees and no flowers, only grassy meadows and huge ferns. I was there alone, and there was no sign that any human being had ever been there, no roads or houses or telephone lines, or anything. But there were many animals. None of them were the kind that we see upon this earth today. In an adjacent meadow I saw a dinosaur; it did not come near me. Many other animals however did come to me and press themselves against me, looking up at me with joy and light in their eyes. I would pick up some big ugly thing, for most of them were big brown clumsy-looking creatures, and would hug it and kiss it; how I loved them, these living creatures coming to greet me! They loved me too. We did not communicate in words (indeed I never hear in dreams; I only see) but I could feel their joy and their love as they crowded around me. Then I sensed them saying, but not in words, "We don't want you to go away because we are afraid that you will step over into Happy Valley."

I do not call heaven "Happy Valley," but I knew that they meant heaven. So I said, "Don't be afraid. It will be a long time before I am due to step over into Happy Valley."

Then I awoke, but even now I am filled with joy when I think of this dream, and I know that whatever it may have meant to my subconscious mind, the real meaning of it was to tell my spirit something about the many mansions of heaven. Can it be that after a time of rest by the "still waters" and of rejoicing before the throne of grace, we may be asked to go to some new planet that has never even heard of Jesus and to take them His love?

Would we be willing to leave the glory of the Holy City and go and minister for a while to those who have never known Christ, upon a planet that is not this earth? This in no way refers to reincarnation, in which I positively do not believe. I believe that we are born only once on this earth. Maybe it is only my missionary forbears that cause me to wonder about the possibility of our going to serve the Lord on other planets, and certainly it is not necessary for you to think about it unless it gives you joy. It does give me joy. It makes heaven seen to me not like floating vaguely about on a rosy cloud, playing a harp and singing hymns, which after a while must become rather stale! It makes me see the next stage of existence as a great adventure, sometimes adoring my Lord Jesus before His throne of light, and at other times going on a mission for Him to some far planet that has never known His love. Again I stress that I am not speaking of reincarnation. In the dream I was not anywhere upon this planet earth. Rather, I was, whether in the flesh or spirit, I know not, but God knoweth, on a very new planet in another solar system, taking the love of Christ to those living beings who were there.

Once I asked Edith Drury, my friend, if she would be willing, if Jesus asked her to do so, to go to a completely new planet and start life there, rather like Eve. Edith responded, "Yes, if Gary Cooper could be Adam!" This has no deep spiritual significance. I only mention it because it is fun!

Anyway, to come back to this planet, and high time too, we have been given a job to do here for our Lord. It is to pray and work for the coming of the kingdom of heaven here on this earth. "Thy kingdom come, thy will be done, on earth as it is in heaven." We had better get on with it.

We have learned in praying for healing that the most important part of the prayer is to give thanks that it has been answered, to accept it by faith, and from then on to see ourselves or the ones for whom we prayed well and perfect. In many of my other books I have discoursed on the fact that if we pray for God to make Emma well, and then say to friends and neighbors, "Poor Emma; isn't it terrible how she suffers!" then our prayers for her are null and void, because while we have asked for her healing, we have not accepted it by faith.

Jesus did not tell us specifically to pray for Emma, though in general ways He surely did suggest that we pray for the recovery of the sick. But He did tell us specifically, in the prayer that He gave us, to pray for the healing of this earth, that it might become a kingdom of heaven. So in order to let this prayer be a real prayer of faith, we should always follow it by saying or thinking, "Thank you, God. You are making this earth into the kingdom of heaven!" And when we hear of sad, frightening things—threatened war in one area of the world or another, for instance—then we should hold up that area to God's light, and pray that His power may overshadow it and that war may be averted, and thus that many lives may be saved.

In other words, and to use modern language, to hear of such a danger and simply say that oh well, it doesn't matter, because Jesus is coming soon, is a sort of holy cop-out. How much better it would be to let the light of God shine on the threatened area through our prayers and see war averted, as three women did in the Cathedral of Notre Dame.

And if you want something really sensational to think about, I suggest that you think about the kingdom of heaven. "Thy will be done on earth as it is in heaven."

What is heaven really like—or one of the heavens—for in our Father's house are "many mansions" (John 14:2). St. John has told us of seeing heaven in the spirit—the New Jerusalem, he called it—and has given us some quite definite but rather puzzling pictures of it. Now if St. John could have visions, so can we, if only we will keep quiet long enough to see them.

I have had glimpses of the New Jerusalem during my prayer time. As I mentioned before, I sometimes hear within me the Lord's voice saying, "Come on up!" which sounds rather casual for so great a deity, but is more my language than, "Come up hither," would be. I wait then in expectancy to see what He will show me, after first calling for the protection of Jesus Christ to be around me while my spirit ventures whither He wishes me to go. I am not asleep when this happens. I am sitting in the chair in my study, just waiting. I am not in a trance or anything like that, but I do close my eyes, the better to see what He is showing my spirit.

The New Jerusalem is very much as St. John described it, I find, only the streets are not solid gold, though they look like gold. When one walks on them it is like walking in a shining golden mist. There really is a river, the river of life, and when my angel stepped into it one time—. Oh, but I haven't told you about my angel. I use the possessive pronoun because he seems to be the one to greet me. At first I did not see any angels; I find that my perception increases as I think about heaven. If we stop letting our imagination brood on great persecutions and tortures and the like, and turn it toward God and His heavens, new doors will open to our minds, new and very thrilling doors, and as we step through those doors in our imagination, I believe we will be healed of any fear or uneasiness we may ever have had about death.

St. John said that the foundation of the walls of the city was made of rubies and emeralds and all kinds of shining jewels. Quite true; they do shine with those rainbow colors, but it is not as if the jewels were set in them by a jeweler, and I am sure that John did not mean it thus. It is that the colors merge into one another as the brilliant light of heaven merges into the lower light of earth, making rainbow colors.

I am not telling you these things with the idea that you too must learn to see the heavens! I just agree with Paul's thought in Philippians 4:8, "Finally, brethren, whatsoever things are true, whatsoever things are pure, whatsoever things are lovely, whatsoever things are of good report; if there be any virtue, and if there be any praise, think on these things."

The thing on which we fasten our minds tends to become true. That is an inexorable rule that cannot be altered. For instance, if we pray for the healing of a friend and then continue to see that person lying on a bed of illness, moaning and groaning, there is no power in the prayer. The picture that we see in our minds takes precedence over the prayer and renders it of no avail.

Similarly, when we pray the Lord's prayer, "Thy kingdom come, thy will be done on earth as it is in heaven," and yet see great tribulation coming upon the earth, and people being persecuted and tortured, we are denying and making of no avail the great prayer that Jesus wanted us to pray. We are actually canceling out by our denial of good and our insistence on evil the very intention of our Lord.

Some people tend to reject immediately any further advance in knowledge of this universe lest it detract from the glory of Jesus, but it does not! Rather, it increases His glory and causes us to adore Him more and more! If, for instance, the guess of astronomers is right that there are probably living beings on other planets than this earth, then Jesus is Lord of *all* of them. He is the main channel of God's love toward God's creation. "All things were made by him; and without him was not anything made that was made. In him was life; and the life was the light of men" (John 1:3-4). That means all "men," from the farthest galaxy to the nearest star and to any planets that may rotate around them.

A problem does arise at this point. If human or humanoid beings exist on other planets, and if they lose the light of God as men on this earth lost it until Jesus came and gave His life for us, then would He have to go to other planets and die again? No! As St. Paul said, "Christ being raised from the dead dieth no more; death hath no more dominion over him" (Rom. 6:9). His redemption accomplished on this earth opens the way for God's light anywhere in the universe of stars and planets and whatever other heavenly bodies there may be. He is Lord of all! He is King of kings, and Lord of lords, and of His kingdom there shall be no end. So if we are willing to broaden our vision of the universe, we are also broadening our comprehension of the glory of Jesus!

C.S. Lewis called this "the visited planet" because the Son of God once came to this planet and gave His life. For whom? For all mankind, wherever they are and in whatever form they may appear. This being the visited planet, we have a joyful duty toward the rest of creation. Jesus told His disciples to go into all the world, and preach the gospel to every creature. This staggers the imagination. All the world? All the universe? Every creature? He did not simply say "every man." I do not think that He meant for us simply to go outdoors and preach the gospel to the birds, as St. Francis did, sweet though that loving deed might be. Why did He say "creature" instead of simply saying "person"? We do not know, for we have not yet seen those beings, sentient beings, whom He called "creatures." Apparently St. John saw them in a vision, as we read in the last book of the Bible, Revelation. Much of it sounds like science fiction, doesn't it! Certainly those queer-looking beings that, together with earth-man, surrounded the throne of God, did not come from this planet! St. John shrewdly guessed that men would boggle at his mysteries and doubt his book about them, and rather crossly he ended his book with warning to those who might be tempted to add to, or take away from, what he had written. He was merely saying firmly, "Now the things that I have written in this book are true, and you'd better believe them." Some people think he was referring to the whole Bible, but that cannot be, for when he wrote this, the Bible had not as yet been compiled out of the documents then circulating among the churches.

How can we "go . . . into all the world and preach the gospel to every creature"? Are we not fixed on this earth? I have no answer to that, unless from the heavens and the heaven of heavens through the long reaches of eternity He sends us out sometimes to be missionaries for Him in far places. That would make of eternity a glorious adventure, whereas the grim picture, held by believers in reincarnation, of simply being born again and again upon this earth would be dismal beyond words, and the picture of standing with a lot of angels singing, "Holy, holy, holy!" forever might pall upon us after a while.

In order to fulfill our glorious heritage upon this earth we need the light of God, and all that we can hold of it. In God is the fountain of life, and that life is our light. If we lack this light of His joy, we can learn to have it! We are so made that the light of God can shine in us. We are, I constantly teach, like light bulbs made on purpose to receive power and project light. We have, or are, not only conscious mind and unconscious mind living together in one body, but we are also spirit. The fixture for receiving God's Holy Spirit is within us, as the fixture for giving electric light may be in a house, and yet the house remains in darkness because the fixture has not been connected with the power flowing from the powerhouse. We are like that. Many of us have prepared the way for the light of God to be turned on in us; we have been baptized and received into a church, and we have asked for the forgiveness of sins and all the rest of it. Yet sometimes we walk in darkness, and within us is an old sadness, and a longing for something, we know not what. I would guess that in most cases it is a longing for the light of God to abide in us through His Holy Spirit, turning all our sorrow into joy, and all our darkness into light.

As I have written elsewhere, and as is commonly known, two or three gathered together can lay their hands upon the head of one desiring an increase and explosion, as it were, of God's Holy Spirit within, praying that it will come. It should never be forced by those who pray, however! In fact, God's Holy Spirit can never be forced! If the ability to speak in tongues, for instance, is insisted upon until a bit of a babble comes from the lips of the seeker, I am not at all sure that this is from God. It may be only a weak imitation of the "real thing," coming from the seeker's subconscious. As a matter of fact, I never pray particularly for the gift of tongues, but rather for the invasion and increase of God's Spirit within the person, bringing forth whatever gifts are best for him or her. However, to be quite frank, it pleases me when tongues do come. We are all human enough to be happy with a bit of evidence, though we should not insist upon it. In any case the gift of tongues is not, if it comes to us, nearly *all* that the Spirit can do within us. We would be wise not to run shouting to everyone that we have received the Holy Spirit, but to guard each precious gift in holy silence at the beginning, while waiting to see what the Holy Spirit will give us next. Light, always light, must be what we most desire, and that invisible light of God is also, or contains also, the joy of the Lord!

This joy is a holy joy, and it should be enshrined in our hearts and kept in reverence, so that it will increase and fill our beings, our homes, and (please God!) our churches.

Let us take this holy joy in our hearts into the churches which we attend, and sit there quietly praying for God's joy to fill the church more and more. Let us pray for healing for those with us in the congregation, and for the enlightenment of the minister—if we feel that he could use some enlightenment! Many of us do feel that, and with some reason, because we may have gifts of the Spirit that he apparently does not have, but if we wait quietly, and pray for him faithfully, he can expand more and more into God's image, in which he is made and for which he seeks. On the other hand, if we make ourselves obnoxious to our minister, by talking out of turn or even by walking around with our noses in the air, as if saying, "We have something that you don't have!" we may just turn him against us, rather than toward the Holy Spirit.

To receive the Holy Spirit is not the end and aim of our striving, but rather it should be to give His light to others, and to our church and nation and world. It cannot, I repeat, be forced.

Someone may come to us and say, "You've got something that I don't have, and I want it because—" Words usually falter here. They may finish, "Because you look so happy," but that is not really the fullness of what they want to say. It is really because with the eyes of the Spirit they see the light that is within us, and what they want is God. "Light is sown for the righteous, and gladness for the upright in heart" (Ps. 97:11). Then we can pray for them with joy for the gift of the Holy Spirit.

It is easier, however, to give this Holy Spirit, this light of God through the spirit of Jesus Christ, to the earth than to people. The earth is always waiting, as it were, for this increase of the light of God that will bring forth all its creativity.

Can the earth perceive the light of God, you may ask? Of course it can! From that light and by that light, the earth came into being, and it seems to sense when that light is violated and turned into darkness. We read in Genesis 4 of the murder of Abel by his brother Cain, and how the Lord said to Cain, "The voice of thy brother's blood crieth unto me from the ground. . . . When thou tillest the ground, it shall not henceforth yield unto thee her strength; a fugitive and a vagabond shalt thou be in the earth" (vv. 10,12).

So it was. The earth lost its fertility because the light of God which had nourished it was darkened by the sin of Cain. The earth itself felt the evil of this deed. Our earth and the houses built upon it at times still feel the evil and sorrow of those who have tilled it, or lived within them. This is no psychic revelation or anything of that sort; it is just plain fact, corroborated by the Bible from beginning to end, and people have understood it throughout history. In my childhood, for instance, the Chinese used to tie the green branch of a tree upon the roof of a new house, in order to protect it. This is why a new church is blessed or consecrated, that the light of Christ may shine into it, driving away all sin and darkness.

When my husband was an active priest he was often asked by

his church families to bless their houses, praying that God's light be increased therein. This was especially done if they had moved into a newly-built house, or one new to them. Thereafter they could feel the light, and know the peace and power of the Lord in their homes. All through church history there have been similar customs, especially the blessing of the fields on Rogation Sunday, when priests and people would march to all the fields around the village church, blessing each one.

When I moved to California in order to be nearer to my children, and also to be handy to the San Andreas Fault in order to pray for it, I looked for a house. My Christian real estate agent knew all along that I would buy this house which is now mine, but she first showed me some others, so that I would recognize "my" house by contrast when I saw it. One of those houses had such a dark, cold atmosphere that I would not even walk into it. From the front door I could feel evil or sorrow, I did not know which. If the family had not been in residence I probably would have suggested going from room to room and blessing that house, asking God to increase His light all through it. But one could hardly rush upon a strange family with such a suggestion!

There is nothing new or strange in the idea of blessing land or houses. The Bible is full of it. Jacob said that Esau smelled like "a field which the Lord hath blessed" (Gen. 27:27). God put His light around the Israelites' houses, when they marked those houses by the blood of a lamb upon the doorposts, and no harm could come to them, even when the angel of death swept through the land.

So I am not telling you anything new when I suggest that you pray for your farm, your garden, your town or city, your country. You might enjoy looking in your Bible, with the help of a concordance, for all the references to the invocation of God's light upon places, just as upon persons.

But if we simply say the words, and do not believe, then of

course nothing happens. I have written many books urging people to acquire and use the power of faith, of belief that something is happening, in cases of illness. Now I am writing this book to suggest to you the power of faith in praying for the kingdom of heaven on earth, for the healing of our fields and farms so that famine will not come, for the healing of our winds and weather so that storms may not destroy crops or people, for the healing of the San Andreas and other faults and tense regions of the earth, for the healing of the minds of men so that they will not continue to set off atomic explosions which cannot help upsetting the earth. The least modicum of common sense would indicate to us that such explosions must disturb and upset the earth. After all, we cannot set off even the smallest bomb in a house without disturbing it.

When I pray for the San Andreas Fault, that it settle its differences, or make its adjustments to the earth that is even now being gradually pushed up from the ocean, I see with the eyes of faith God's healing and constructive power, God's life-force of light, shining into the mountains beneath which the fault lurks, and causing these areas of new land to develop so gently, so gradually, that there shall be no destructive earthquakes. Many people, encouraged by the newspapers, seem to gloat in the prospect of a destructive earthquake, and to delight in foretelling it. However, God is more powerful than all newspapers and gloomy prophets who foresee calamity.

So, I call upon God's light. And I call upon Jesus Christ, the Son of God who shed His blood upon this earth that it might be cleansed of the sins of its people and become the kingdom of God, or one of the kingdoms of God in this universe. Then I see with the eyes of faith God's light channeled through Jesus and entering into these tense areas, releasing the tension, melting down with His light any dangerous pressures as new land comes to birth, and so establishing this area in peace and gentleness.

We used to say, "You bet your life. . . ." Well, so I do.

In this prayer it helps me to understand what the earth and its Creator are trying to do in earthquakes, and I have learned much from an inventor friend who knows, I should think, everything there is to know about earthquakes and has invented ways of constructing buildings to make them safe in even major quakes. And where did this man of science get the knowledge enabling him to do these feats of engineering? He learned from prayerful study of the earth, and its manner of growing, and I have listened to him gladly on many occasions.

The earth as we see it, neatly covered with grass and trees, or in some areas sand, is only about forty miles deep. The earth's center, once considered to be solid, is now thought by scientists to be a raging furnace of boiling, exploding metallic substance. The earth, we might say, is made of fire, and the fire is building an earth just as though it knew what it is doing; it's Creator, God, does know, for the earth is His creature. How amazing that St. Paul so long ago by God's inspiration called it the "creature" (according to the King James Version)! As the metallic substances begin to cool, they harden, and so the fiery center is surrounded with a metallic shell on which the earth as we know it has been built. This shell is not in one piece but in four irregular parts, like an orange, the skin of which peels off in four jagged pieces. Two of these parts, according to the experts, happen to press on each other in the area of Southern California, tending to press the land upwards as they do so. In the recent San Fernando earthquake the mountains, I was told, rose nine inches. That really builds new land. On the East Coast, by contrast, the land is sinking and the mountains are old and smooth, crowned with rocks worn round by the ages.

None of this is new information. Many of us probably learned it in about the fifth grade. But I didn't, for I never attended any grades, excepting for a few months once when we were at home on furlough from China, and I was bored absolutely to extinction! I had been used to studying the assignments my mother gave me up in the old elm tree with the crows. Not many of the crows were at home in the mornings actually. It was more fun at sunset time when they flew cawing from the city wall and went to bed in the old elm tree!

At any rate, there is nothing new in the fact that the West Coast of the United States is one of the continuing acts of God's creation. Therefore it would not be wise to pray that all earthquakes cease, for how then would the land grow? Rather, I have learned to pray that there may be as many small tremors as necessary for growth, but no great smashing ones.

Does the earth hear me? Of course it hears me and all who pray for it, though not with ears! God's hands are still upon the earth, creating. And though there are only a few tiny voices, mine and the others who love the earth, still the power goes forth from God to the earth. The earth responds because this prayer is made in faith, and faith is the very active energy of God in motion.

Unfortunately, the earth may also be somewhat responsive to those who at times run away from earthquake-prone areas. They run away when they hear prophecies of an earthquake, instead of staying and praying with faith for the earth to be protected. I am sure that the energy of the prayer of faith can overcome the weaker energy of fear, and if only all Christians would stay and pray instead of running away the task would not be so great for any of us.

CHAPTER 5

As I write this morning the rain is softly falling over the mountains, enfolding my orchids, oleanders, and whole garden in a gentle mist. This is an unexpected rain. The newspaper on my driveway was soaking wet, and that never happens, for when rain is foretold by the weather experts, they then enclose it in a plastic cover. This is a prayed-for rain, out of season and very much needed.

Who can pray for rain or for sunshine contrary to forecasts, and have the prayers answered? Those who love the earth and believe in God. They are able to speak from the heart to the heart of the earth we live upon, and to God, the Creator of the earth.

It is rather hard to believe that God can hear such prayers, and most people would think it impossible that the earth can be aware of prayer going forth for its healing and comfort. But it can! After all, God created this earth, and what material did He have out of which to make it? Only His own word! Only His own glory! When He said, "Let there be light!" it appeared out of darkness, and from that light the universe was made. Until He sent forth the word, the earth was "without form, and void"

(Gen. 1:2). Therefore within the earth, as in the whole of creation, there is an awareness of God the Creator. The earth can feel God's love and respond to prayer.

The Bible is full of this! As the Lord said to Habakkuk, "For the earth shall be filled with the knowledge of the glory of the LORD, as the waters cover the sea" (2:14). "Let the heavens be glad, and let the earth rejoice: and let men say among the nations, The LORD reigneth" (1 Chron. 16:31). "As for the earth, out of it cometh bread: and under it is turned up as it were fire" (Job 28:5). "The LORD reigneth; let the earth rejoice; let the multitude of isles be glad thereof" (Ps. 97:1).

In the Episcopal Book of Common Prayer also we have numerous similar references: "In His hands are all the corners of the earth, and the strength of the hills is His also. Oh, worship the Lord in the beauty of holiness; let the whole earth stand in awe of Him." "All the earth doth worship thee, oh Father everlasting."

But surely, you may think, this means all the people who live upon the earth, not the earth itself. I do not think so, and if it did, He could say so. Lest any want to restrict praise to people, one of the canticles sometimes used in Morning Prayer in the Episcopal Church includes these delightful verses: "O ye Mountains and Hills, bless ye the Lord: praise him and magnify him for ever. O all ye Green Things upon the earth. . . . O ye wells. . . . O ye seas and floods. . . . O ye whales. . . . O all ye Fowls of the air. . . . O all ye beasts and cattle. . . . O ye children of men. . . ." Each follow with the refrain: "Bless ye the Lord: praise him and magnify him for ever."

Plainly to those who compiled the Book of Common Prayer the life of God so permeates this world that from earth and sea, from birds of the air and creatures of the deep, arises a song without words, an emanation of joy and love to the Creator! It is thrilling to my soul to sing this anthem, long and repetitious as it is. We can almost hear all the creatures that it speaks of, and if we are at all aware of the natural world around us there comes from within us too a sense of joy and wonder and praise to the God who made this world by His word of power, from the outskirts of His glory, that He may enjoy and cherish it, and that it may enjoy and cherish Him forever.

If we know that "The earth is the Lord's, and the fulness thereof" (Ps. 24:1), then we can pray for the earth, that it may be saved from "earthquake, fire and flood," as the Prayer Book says, and we can know that our prayers of faith will be answered—that is, if we are prepared in ourselves. "If my people, which are called by my name, shall humble themselves, and pray, and seek my face, and turn from their wicked ways; then will I hear from heaven, and will forgive their sin, and will heal their land" (2 Chron. 7:14). Thus the Lord spoke to Israel, God's experimental race, the people chosen to "inherit the earth." All the prophecies about the Lord's Second Coming were made to Israel. We assume that they were the pilot race, as it were, to show the way to God, and that what He said to them He said to all who call upon His name. Certainly if we unhesitatingly claim the gloomy prophecies for ourselves, we can also claim these happy ones! Moreover, we can bring the happy promises more surely and quickly to life if we rejoice in the Lord and in His creation, rather than moaning over it and looking forward to its destruction! Joy gives power to prayer; sorrow weakens it. The prayer of desperation is not so powerful as the prayer of joyous expectancy.

Let us rejoice, therefore, in fields that shine with the glory of God, and in mountains snow-capped that lift their heads to honor Him! Let us delight in knowing that His way is on the far seas and that thundering waves rise and crash at His feet to honor Him. Honor and glory are His forever. Before the earth came out of the sea, He is, the ever-living One. He is the king of glory, and the Lord of life, and in Him there is no death nor shadow of the grave. He is the king of joy, and His joy rises into the singing of delight in great things and in small! Let us rejoice therefore in the mockingbirds that sing throughought the night when all save them is still! Let us rejoice in rattlesnakes who withhold their sting from those who love them and who love the Lord! In wind and rain let us rejoice, and in the snow of winter covering the earth with shining whiteness, and in the summer sun that brings forth life from the soil.

Let us rejoice! The whole Bible is full of this refrain which is also a command: Rejoice! As we rejoice in Him our homes will become more and more places of peace, so that those who are sad and weary will delight in entering our doors. And another thing will happen: we will grieve for those whose natural fountain of joy is muddied over with resentments, and dried up with grief, and we will long to lead them also into the light of the Lord. I am not at the moment speaking of converting outsiders to Christianity, but of praying for converted believers who do not yet live in the joy of the Lord. I myself know whereof I speak. Having accepted Christ as a small child, and having lived all my life in the most rigid orthodoxy and the most firm belief in Him, I did not walk in His joy, but under a heavy cloud of depression until a minister of the church finally prayed for me, not that I should be converted, but that I should walk in the joy of the Lord.

The crown and glory of our individual, personal prayers is the great privilege of sending forth the light to the world, even as the sun sends forth light into this whole galaxy.

Can we do so? I do not feel any power in this kind of prayer when I try to pray for the whole universe, or even for this planet on which we live. But when I reduce the area of my prayer to a city, or sometimes a larger or smaller area, then I can feel the light-energy of God go through me, and before too long I can ascertain the results of it in the area for which I have prayed.

"But this prayer is too big for me," you may be thinking, "even if I narrow it down to a city or a town."

Well then, I say, narrow it down even more, and pray first of all for your own home!

No one, I am sure, found uplift in my home when I was walking in darkness, even though I always did my best to take care of three little children and do all the housework. Later on, however, when I began to find my way to peace, people would step inside the front door and say something like, "What is it? I always feel better when I come into this house." It was the peace of God they felt, even sometimes amid the sound of children playing, or the sloshing of the washing machine.

All of us can learn to have this peace by lifting up our spirits to God as soon as possible in the morning and keeping them there, and by making the homes in which we live a reflection of that peace. It can be so that whenever a stranger enters, he will say that just to come in makes him feel good somehow. It is the peace of God that can be felt, and we can achieve it by lifting up our souls to God the very first chance we can get, and there abiding until His peace enters us and overflows into us and our households.

In the old days I could not do this until the baby was fed and put down for his nap, and the other children had gone off to school or kindergarten. I no longer live among pattering footsteps and chattering babies, and from the distance of many years I will tell all adoring and befuddled mothers that there is a prize for growing old, and it is the gift of peace. In the old days, when the baby was asleep, and the other children were absorbing learning (I hoped), I would slip away into the church for my morning prayer-and-listening time. Today I do not need to go out of my own house, for it is filled with the peace of God.

If the Lord is to abide in my house, then the home must be worthy of Him. I am not one to go around peering under sofas looking for dust, but I am one who, loving Jesus, wishes for no discordant note in my home which is also His home. It should be filled with the peace of serene beauty, as well as with the peace of prayer. My furniture is mostly old and somewhat battered, but it is not discordant; no color screams at another color, no article of furniture is so bizarre as to catch the eye with an unpleasant jolt. There are flowers in my house, for they live and breathe the beauty of God, and without them the house would feel lifeless. I do not mean plastic flowers! Never, by the grace of God, plastic flowers! Mine must be real, breathing forth life in their tiny way, even as God breathes forth His life.

All the pictures on my walls, and there are many, are of the peace and the glory of God caught and translated into mountains and ocean, woods and cliffs and running brooks. Most of them I have painted myself. I studied art in college, for which I am most grateful, and find that the creation of beauty in pastels, bringing forth on a piece of plain paper the glory of the earth, is one of the most joyous ways of serving God, of helping to bring forth His kingdom. In defense of God's gift of painting, I must add that I am professional, and now selling my pictures for prices in three figures. Some may find this a rude shock, since it may contradict the concept of me as a person continually on her knees praying for someone (preferably you), or some good cause. No! I am not that kind of person! And I doubt whether such a person, unless upheld by the life of a monastic community, can bring healing to very many people. The spirit becomes weary when one keeps on forcing it. Prayer is a creative impulse, but one needs to rest the creative impulse for a while, and it is rested by turning to another form of creativity. In painting and gardening I find my special refreshment from my times of prayer.

If at all possible we who are serious about the life of prayer, that ever-flowing prayer which is the gift of the Spirit, should have one room kept for prayer only. I know that sometimes this is not possible, but it is the ideal. In the old baby-rearing days I would escape every morning for a little while and go into the church, which in time became so Spirit-filled that some people could see the light of the Lord therein.

Nowadays I have my own study which is also my prayer room. It is wonderful to have this quiet place where nothing is ever done except prayer and meditation. Merely social visits can be held in the living room. The study is my own place, and none shall enter here except for prayer. Even my painting is done upstairs on the dining room table.

I have already, in chapter 2, described in some detail how I start each day in meditation, or rather prayer-and-listening. Again I stress the danger in the term "meditation" because to so many people it suggests some form of non-Christian meditation, transcendental and otherwise, which allows the spirit to be lifted into the unknown, with willingness to catch and bring back anything that it picks up. This can be dangerous, especially for those who call themselves Christians. For us, to be "spiritual" without Jesus is as dangerous as climbing a steep mountain in the dark without a light. I do not say it is wicked, and I know a few Christian people who can apparently get by with it, but I do say that it is dangerous. One can be led astray, or even possessed by spirits other than the Spirit of Jesus, and this is death to the soul. "But meditation is all very spiritual!" you may say. So is Satan very spiritual. He is a spiritual being, not clothed in flesh, but he is dangerous. So my prayer of protection is the most important part, the absolutely necessary preliminary, to any of my meditations.

Following that, Jesus, or His Holy Spirit, has shown me great things wherein I rejoice even while being a little bit afraid or in awe. He has shown me life and the continuance of life, heaven and the heavens, so that I positively know that we go from glory to glory, from life to life in the heavens, never again on this earth. When I see glimpses of this heaven or that, I see that they are not a state of being in which one floats around in six or seven dimensions. I could never understand that! Heaven is a place! Do I see Jesus there? No, not immediately, not in the nearer heavens. By nearer, I mean those that are more like this earth, Paradise possibly. The one that I assume is nearer (at least in time if not in space, of which I know nothing) is not too different from this earth. There I seem to be in a wide valley with low, blue hills in the distance. The valley is filled with flowers. None of them are exactly the same flowers that I see on this earth; they are brighter and more beautiful, more distinct with life somehow. I cannot quite explain this, but it seems as if the life shines out of them; one can see them living and growing.

No, I have not seen Jesus there. At first I saw no living being at all. Some months later on I saw the angel who usually shows up in whatever stage of heaven my soul is wandering. He is tall and very beautiful. I say "he," for while I know that angels are neither masculine nor feminine, he seems more like a man than a woman. (The simpering female angels so often pictured on greeting cards give me furiously to doubt!) I do not remember that he spoke to me at all in this bit of a vision of the nearer heaven—or at least I assume it is a nearer heaven because it is so much more like this earth. It might be the reality and this earth a copy of it—a poorer, dimmer copy. As I have already told, on other occasions I have been, in the spirit, within the walls of the New Jerusalem which St. John evidently also beheld. I saw the golden streets and the river of life, but there seemed to be no one on those streets. I asked the angel in thought, for we communicated only in that way, why I didn't see any people there. He replied, "Because these have not yet attained to the resurrection of the body. Therefore it would not be safe for you to see them."

Wow! Or perhaps I should say, "Hallelujah!" This gives us all much food for thought, and I am not going to tell you what I think either. God can tell us each what He likes about it.

On another occasion I was lifted up in spirit, but I was not unconscious. I knew that my body was sitting right here in the study. But another part of me beheld a great white throne and

Him that sat upon it. All I could see really was a tremendous sunburst of white light, and somehow I knew that it proceeded out of the throne of God, and on that throne was the Son of God in glory everlasting. At a little distance I saw a group of people all radiant in white raiment, and I perceived that they were people, not angels. "Who are these?" I asked the angel, in thought only, you understand.

He said, "These are they which . . . have washed their robes, and made them white in the blood of the Lamb" (Rev. 7:14). In other words, they had attained their resurrection bodies. That was why I could "see" them in the vision. Maybe he was quoting from the Book of Revelation of St. John, or maybe both he and St. John were quoting from the direct word of God.

It may seem strange that intermingled in this book about praying for this earth you find bits about heaven. It is because I am older than I once was, and as I draw nearer to heaven I begin to see the light of it. In that light pictures of it come and go, and sometimes I "see" those pictures not from afar but from within. I find it very enjoyable.

However, the seeing of bits of truth not of this world is not the final purpose of my prayer-listening time. The real purpose is to do the work that God has given me to do. That is more important than any number of visions. Therefore, I never come up, as it were, out of my prayer time without asking for guidance and strength to do whatever He wants me to do that day.

So let us come back now from the heaven and the heaven of heavens to this little earth. It may be a bit boring after our far excursions, but it is where we live now, and where we are ordered to show forth His power, building here a kingdom of peace. As we pray, "Thy kingdom come, thy will be done on earth as it is in heaven," we are supposed to believe it, to have faith, as we are told in the Bible time after time. It is difficult! We began by working and praying for peace in our own homes, so that we can find there a fit place in which to pray and listen to God.

Now let us choose one bit of the great world, and extend our believing prayer beyond our home. It may be a place of business, a town, or church, or school. I suggest that you consider taking one particular schoolroom as your next project. It is smaller and easier to encompass with faith than a whole school would be, or a whole town, and many of us have children or grandchildren in school, and we are concerned for them, quite rightly. Satan does seem to be carrying on his perennial warfare on this earth by particularly attacking our schools. I said above that I feel that the "great persecution" is past; but the war is not over and Satan is still with us, and will be to the end. When we meet the enemy we are not told meekly to submit to him but, "Resist the devil, and he will flee from you" (James 4:7).

So let us each choose one schoolroom to begin with, and let us rebuke Satan and command him in the name of Jesus to flee out of that room, taking with him all violence and evil. Note that the prayer does not end here however. We must next picture in our minds that schoolroom, seeing it full of loving kindness and the joy of learning. Let us picture the goodness of the Lord shining forth in it like a light, so that the young people find there the things that are good, and only things that are good. We are picturing this so that it may become so in the future. However, we know that at the present time a great deal of prayer is needed, and whatever action the Lord may guide us to undertake. We know that in spite of everything, drugs are still available in most schools, bringing all their devastating effects, and this must end. In the name of Jesus Christ, say with me now as you read it: *This must end!* Continue to pray the prayer of command, which is the prayer of faith, and to follow it with, "Thank you, Lord. This will end!" And then make the picture in your mind of the school, and the particular room which is your prayer assignment, cleansed and set free from this danger.

Another evil more subtle than drugs which is threatening our schools is the sin of breaking God's commandment of chastity. I know what is actually taught in some schools and colleges because the young people attending them have told me. One of them told me that her psychology teacher said in class: "If you feel desire toward some boy and do not follow it, you are just copping out." Thus many of our young people actually see nothing wrong in living together without marriage. Well, what is wrong with it? What harm does it do? The harm in it is not to the physical but to the spiritual body, as I learned from a wise minister friend. The physical bodies of the two can get up and go their ways. The spiritual bodies cannot. A bond has been made between them so that they are tied to each other inwardly in a way they cannot understand. In attempting to live with that tie upon them they either become hardened by the inner effort of it, or they fall into depression because they cannot free themselves from it. If they do legalize their position by marriage later, then the danger of developing neurotic symptoms is minimized. But if they finally marry someone else, then the former relationship is likely to rise up at some point and trouble them. They can be set free by an act of penitence and confession, preferably with a minister or praying friend who can then pronounce the belief that this prayer for forgiveness is being answered and the person is being set free. But if they are not set free, my minister friend added, this may become a heavy weight that their spirits will have to carry through life. He added that this is much more of a weight to a woman than to a man.

You may be thinking that is not fair! The answer is obvious: God is not fair! He is not interested in standardization. He has in mind one objective: the building of the kingdom on earth, the building of the temple of the Lord, that He may abide in it. No one builds a whole temple out of identical blocks of stone. To grace it the building must have stones of different sizes and shapes, artfully patterned, and beams of wood as well, and windows of glass. God is not interested in making man and woman exactly alike, any more than He makes every tree exactly like every other tree, or every flower equal to every other flower. The principle of equality is not one of the cornerstones of heaven. So in making men and women different, and in making all of us different from each other, God is showing His interest in building His temple on earth.

So what can we do about this situation, this condoning of immorality, aside from ourselves living according to His commandments, which I trust we endeavor to do? We can change it by prayer, as I have said before. We really can!

But that is too big for us! It is too large an order! Certainly; so it is! Therefore let us each take one schoolroom, especially if we have a spiritual entry there through a child or grandchild. And let us pray the prayer of faith for that one room, that the light of the Lord will shine in it, and the righteousness of God be manifest in it, and that it be so filled with His holy loving kindness that no evil can enter into it. This is not too hard, and I challenge you to try it. But tell no one! Some prayers work better in secrecy. Hence Jesus often told those whom He healed to, "See thou tell no man; but go thy way" (Matt. 8:4).

All of this may sound very difficult, but it is not so hard as you may think. I will give you a new concept of this kind of prayer, though in reality it is an old concept. Think of God's presence and power in the room you have chosen to pray for as a light, a light of such high radiance and such fine wavelength that it cannot be seen by the human eye. The light of radium or x-ray is of this nature.

In addition to this unknown light that comes from somewhere in our universe, there is also the light of God which is before all and beyond all and within all. This light of God is as real as the light of x-ray, and even more powerful. "The Lord shall be thine everlasting light," said Isaiah (60:20).

Very well then; through Jesus our Lord this light is available to us. Because it dwells with God (Dan. 2:22), through God it shines into us, and through us into the earth around us. Therefore we can direct this light of God into a certain schoolroom, for instance, and it will abide there and increase more and more. We direct it by prayer and faith, not into the teacher, for she might reject it, nor into the students already set on an evil course, for they would not accept it. People have free will, but empty space does not have free will, nor do material things such as doors and walls. So let us see by faith this invisible yet powerful light of God filling the schoolroom, so that its atmosphere changes to one of lightness, joy and peace. This is a great miracle, but it can happen in the schoolroom, a business office, anywhere. Many instances of answered prayer of this kind have been related to me. More than one office has been changed by it, so that the employees feel happy about going there, instead of dreading each day's work. Certainly! The light of God through just one person's faithful prayers can permeate any room or place of work, filling it with a radiation or vibration of love.

You may be thinking: "Well then, why don't we just pray for every classroom, and every school, and—?"

Hold up! Do not run away with this idea. We already pray the great overall prayer in the affirmation, "Thy kingdom come!" This little prayer I have suggested for one schoolroom is to lay a single stone, as it were, into the edifice of His kingdom, which obviously is not yet built. But we will build it by His power and His name, stone by stone. You see, when we pray for His light to fill a schoolroom, we are offering ourselves as channels for that light; we are praying that our light, of Him and through Him, shall go and fill that room. We are the branches on which His fruit of love and joy and peace may grow, remember? We are the light bulbs through whom the eternal light of His shining may enter into one classroom and change its atmosphere, filling it with His peace. Isn't that an exciting thing? "Yes, if it's only true," I can feel you thinking. Well, try it and see if it is true! You

83

don't stand beside a light fixture hour after hour wondering if it will work; you try it and see! So, choose your classroom, and then imagine an invisible radiation of God's light entering that room and filling it with the gentleness of God's love. Now don't go overboard and imagine all the students turning immediately into saints! Keep your mind on the *room*, and on God's light filling it with a glow of gentleness and loving kindness and joy. Pray this once every morning, and occasionally throughout the day when the school comes into your mind. You will be surprised! No, you won't be surprised, because you know it will happen!

Now let me suggest another room which may be much nearer to you: a Sunday school room. Maybe you have no connection with a church, though I doubt it. Most people who read my books are church members who are confused or let down because they do not receive in the church the light and life that they need, in which case, having read at least some of my books, why don't they go back to their churches and try to give light rather than just to receive it? Any who do this will probably receive it also, for as we give forth the light of God, that light comes back to us. The very purpose of a church is to be a receiving and transmitting center of the life of God.

If you have children in your family, you will of course be interested in the work of teaching children about God, which is the aim of the church school. First of all, find out what they teach. I would not suggest that you visit a class and sit grimly among them to see whether they are "sound." That would be disconcerting to the teacher. You can probably find out by talking to your children or grandchildren.

You may be somewhat surprised. I know of one church school in which the teachers, despairing of interesting the children in the Bible, just simply taught handicrafts. I admit it is difficult to find teachers who both know and love the Bible and also know and love children. Whey my husband began his rectorship in New Jersey he found the Sunday school very small, taught by well-meaning older ladies who, with all their good intentions, failed to get the idea across. He reorganized the whole church school, employing members of the congregation who were professional teachers, and paying them some small amount each Sunday. The money for these small salaries came from the children, or rather their parents, by the introduction of the envelope system into the church school. The children pledged five cents, or six, or one, as the case might be, and they came with their little envelopes and were much more interested in learning.

Most of you are not ministers, but still I feel guided to pass along these suggestions, which may come in handy in some way. Perhaps you might even go to the minister if you are interested and offer to teach a class. Have a cushion handy, in case he falls in a faint of surprise! But do not make this offer unless you are prepared to study and to teach the *Bible*. It is the Word of God, but it was given to men thousands of years ago, and it needs to be re-thought and often re-expressed to make sense to people, even children, of today. In *The Healing Power of the Bible* I wrote down some of my Bible class lessons, which were for adults, but it might interest you to read them if you haven't.

Whether or not you go to such lengths as to teach in the church school, you can certainly pray for one class in it, in an even more intensified way than for a public school class. Choose if possible a class that one of your children attends. Then imagine Jesus himself in that class, standing with arms outstretched toward the children, as we often see Him in pictures. Then imagine one child after another sensing His presence in some way great or small. One might say to his mother afterwards, "I went to Sunday school, and Jesus was there!" Or he may say nothing and know nothing about your praying, but just complain less as time passes about having to go

85

to Sunday school. He may not understand that the Spirit of Jesus is there in his class but the fact is that you are praying that this holy presence will be there, and Jesus never refuses such an invitation.

"Lo, I am with you alway, even unto the end of the world," Jesus said (Matt. 28:20). When we open a door to Him, into that door He comes.

You see, He was born into this world of a human mother, the blessed Virgin Mary, and He gathered us into himself, and took upon himself all our darkness of evil so that we would be able to shine forth His light into the world. Having done so, He died for us so that His Holy Spirit would forever shine in our world and through His Spirit we ourselves could become light-bearers. It is very difficult to explain this to grown people, let alone children. I have tried to explain it by writing down the story of how this explanation made life new for a little girl. The story is called *Melissa and Her Little Red Book*. I have just received a call from a seminary professor who is delighted with it. So if you are sufficiently interested I think you will find *Melissa* a good commentary on the redemption of our Lord.

The more you understand about the reality of Jesus, the more you will be able to pray for Him to be in the church school classroom. Imagine Him there! Picture Him there! Give thanks that He is there, and that the children and the teacher will be more and more drawn to Him! This can be a fascinating adventure, and I challenge you to try it. In the beginning I suggest that you pray for only one room, that the light of Christ will fill that room, but you do not need to limit your prayers to that. "Why not the whole Sunday school right away?" you may ask. That would be fine if you are able to conduct that much light.

"But God can do anything," you might say. "He can change the whole Sunday school—even the whole church—right away!" Well, try praying for that if you like, and see. If it is changing and being filled with His light, fine. If on the other hand you notice no particular change, remember that He has chosen to work *through us*, and so try something nearer your size; try one room first! Then when one room becomes warm and friendly in feeling, and so filled with His joy that the children love to go there, take on another!

Do you know that if every Christian did this, we would have a new world!

You see, the light has already come into this world. We did not make it nor invent it. It is here, available that we may use it. "The people which sat in darkness saw great light; and to them which sat in the region and shadow of death light is sprung up" (Matt. 4:16).

It was Jesus who brought that light. It is Jesus through whom the light still shines. But it is ourselves, our small inconsequential selves yet great through His greatness, through whom the light shines. "Ye are the light of the world. A city that is set on a hill cannot be hid" (Matt. 5:14).

If you are still not sure that this is true, let me suggest to you the easiest way of finding out: pray for your garden or your house plants, and see how the light of God's love and joy seems to shine back from them to you. I do not go quite so far as the English army chaplain mentioned previously who said that he prayed for his roses, and asked them to pray for him, and yet, something like that does seem to take place. You do not have any growing things? Oh dear, how quite too bad, as the English would say. Then by all means hasten to get them. If you live in an apartment and have no room for a garden, even a geranium or a fern in a stand is better than nothing.

Pray for them, imagining a current of invisible light from God entering into them and blessing them and helping them to grow. Then every morning go into your garden, or sniff your geranium, or bend over your fern to see if it is dry, and listen! Listen not with the ears but with the heart. Maybe at first you will be too self-conscious to feel it, and I don't blame you. It is wise to protect yourself by secrecy, by an air of casualness. You don't want everybody in the office to say, "There's old Jones again, communing with his geranium!"

Some might say, "But shouldn't we be open about these things, so as to testify to the Lord?"

My anwer is, well, no—not unless you want someone to send for the little man in the white coat. And I am mindful of Jesus' sensible words in this regard, recorded in Matthew 7:6, "Give not that which is holy unto the dogs, neither cast ye your pearls before swine. . . ." No, I say worship the Lord in quietness, and be humble enough to love a little flower in His name, and one day you too will feel it for yourself—a quiver of joy, a bit of comfort, the "letting down of the heart," as the Chinese would say, the relief of tension. It is God's light coming to you in a very gentle way through this creature of God's, the garden or the fern or the geranium, that you have tended.

CHAPTER 6

Now let us extend our prayer-power into the world around us. As I am pointing out repeatedly throughout this book, the very first petition that our Lord taught us to pray in His prayer-example which we call the Lord's Prayer is "Thy kingdom come, thy will be done, on earth as it is in heaven." The creation waits for this. "For the creation waits with eager longing for the revealing of the sons of God" (Rom. 8:19). And who are they? Ourselves! For as we unite ourselves with the flow of God's power in the world, as we are led by the Spirit of God, then we become truly His sons and daughters.

However, let us not rush out and tell people so, but let us continue our work of prayer by looking beyond our homes and schools, and praying for the town, or city, or village in which we live. We do not need to kneel upon the steps of the town hall. We can simply go about our business, and as we visit the market and the post office ask the Spirit of God to go in with us and bless the people who work there, as well as all who come in and out, asking God to fill the very building itself with His light. And He will! The light of God is an invisible radiation of goodness and joy, and we are not likely ever to see it in an office or grocery store, but if we listen to our own feelings we can sense it. Others, not expecting it, will not notice, but nevertheless it will breathe a gentle blessing on them as they come in and go out, and the atmosphere of the whole town will gradually change.

I know this because I have experienced it. When we first moved to New Jersey the town felt stiff and cold. I missed the warm friendliness of the South. But gradually, as I learned to pray there, and as God's light increased in me and in the church, the very town took on a different atmosphere.

I have sometimes told of my experiment in forgiveness regarding one of the stores whose owners had seemed to me unkind in failing to deliver a very much needed order as they had said they would do. On realizing this, I set myself to forgive, and to learn to like the owner of that store and his sons. The climax of this adventure in forgiveness came at the Thanksgiving season when I went into the store for my usual small purchases. This time the owner sent one of his sons scurrying for a turkey, then struck his hand on the counter, raised his voice, and made a short speech. "Mrs. Sanford has been a good friend to us," he said, "so now it is my pleasure to present to her this Thanksgiving turkey!" I was deeply grateful. Those were the years in which the purchase of a turkey was not a matter to be approached lightly. It did not occur to any of my husband's placid parishioners to send us a turkey for the holidays, and the minister, they felt, should be kept poor and humble as befitted him. But to this Jewish storekeeper whose vocation included the counting of pennies, the turkey came as an inspiration.

Many of us cherish small grudges against a storekeeper whom we consider negligent, or a garbage man who tends to come late (while visiting dogs ravage the garbage) and we do not realize that our feelings of dislike or annoyance have any spiritual significance. But they do! They block the way of the light. When we remove that block, then the light can shine through us and gradually fill our town so that it is a happy place to visit and a good place to live.

My daughter recently told me that an old friend had come to see her and had said that they had just found the nicest town for their home. They were looking for a place to live near Philadelphia, and came across a lovely little town with a warm and friendly atmosphere, and the most delightful small stone church with a particularly wonderfully warm feeling in it.

"That was my town!" my daughter exclaimed. "My father was rector of that church!" And I might add that the rector who followed him and is still there, and the congregation as well, have kept the spirit of prayer alive in that church.

"The people which sat in darkness saw a great light; and to them which sat in the region and shadow of death light is sprung up" (Matt. 4:16). That was the light of Jesus Christ, our Lord. That light is still among us, only since He has gone to the Father, we are the small conductors of a great light which we are to channel into the world. "Ye are the light of the world," said Jesus. However, let us not say to a storekeeper, or to anyone for that matter, "You know, when I go downtown I *always pray*." It turns people off. They may look at you and say, "My dear, what a wonderful person you are!" but they scuttle out of your way just as fast as they can!

Jesus had much to say on this point. "Beware of the scribes, which love to go in long clothing, and love salutations in the marketplaces . . . and for a pretence make long prayers" (Mark 12:38,40). "But thou, when thou prayest, enter into thy closet, and when thou hast shut the door, pray to thy Father which is in secret; and thy Father which seeth in secret shall reward thee openly" (Matt. 6:6).

Most of our closets are ill adapted for this purpose, but we can go into a bedroom or living room and close the door, and not let our neighbor find us and gush, "How wonderful you are! You just pray all the time, don't you!" We often serve the Lord best in silence, but we can serve Him, even in the streets of our town or city, by loving and praying for and blessing the very streets and houses, until the community becomes more and more filled with His peace.

I do not suggest that we make it a point to study all the affairs of the city, and decide whether or not to vote for new officials. We do not need to know who is on the town council, so as to vote for his successor, unless we just happen to be avidly interested in politics. I do not even advise that we decide so to move the Lord by prayer that He will see that such and such a person is elected. We just might be wrong! I would rather use my energy in prayer, and let the decisions rest with the Lord. (Take note, if you will, that I am speaking without the guidance of my husband who, when he was alive, required me to vote and instructed me carefully. All I had to do was to remember whom he told me to vote for long enough to get down to the fire house!) Of course I do recognize our obligation to vote as wisely as we can, but some things we can more effectively pray for than vote for; that is my point here, especially peace and order in our towns and schools and homes.

What about our state, our country—such enormous areas? Of course we should pray for God's peace for them too, and presumably we do every time we go to church, but while we can after a while see and feel the difference in our town, we cannot always feel and know it in our country, no matter how much we pray. Why? God can do anything, can He not? Why isn't it just as easy for Him to make our whole country safe and happy and good as it is for Him thus to move, according to our prayers, in our town or city? Can't God do everything?

Yes, He could, if He had so chosen, but as the psalmist says, and we have already quoted, He has not so chosen. "The heaven, even the heavens, are the Lord's: but the earth hath he given to the children of men" (Ps 115:16). So we are appointed to take care of this earth. It is our workshop in which to learn of the wisdom and glory of God. It is our vineyard wherein to serve Him and to act as His stewards and helpers. And it is to our eternal joy and glory that this is so! For if we cannot serve Him well on this little planet, how shall we serve Him to His glory in the long reaches of eternity and in heavenly mansions beyond our sight? So, then, He is not going to act unilaterally in small matters such as keeping the peace of our school or town. That is up to us: to act for Him and through Him, and to let Him act through us.

This is not as easy as it might sound, for if we are to be God's agents, then we must positively remain in His love. Storekeepers can be trying, even though for the most part they are wonderfully courteous. Neighbors can be more trying. Their trash can blow into our yard; their dogs can tear up our gardens; their radios can keep us awake at night. All this is very hard, but it is nothing compared to the sins of our Lord's countrymen and contemporaries toward Him. And what did He do? He forgave, and for His sake, so must we. This can be a great adventure if we do it in the privacy of our own minds, never saying to the shoe man, for instance, "Well, you did a very poor job on that shoe, but I forgive you." Never tell anyone that you forgive him! It is an insult. You can ask *him* to forgive *you* if you have sinned against him, though in most cases it is best to say nothing, and just to try to be kind from that time on. But to say that you forgive someone implies, first, that they are in error, which they don't like, and secondly, that you are a wonderful Christian, which they don't like either. There are other ways of letting them know that if you had any dislike it has turned into liking; you don't have to say so!

However, let me not deceive you; this is not always easy. If you are going to pray for a town to be filled with God's light, then you also must be filled with that light. It is all very well to say as we come out of church, with our minds conditioned to holiness, that we are indeed filled with the light of His love. But when we go downtown and a couple of teenage boys roar past us on motorcycles, we may think, "Oh, they have no manners at all. I hope my daughter won't have anything to do with trash like that!" Or as we pass the dentist's office, we may remember how distressful our last visit was, and wonder when we will again have to go through such agony. Or the minister of another denomination may come out of his church, and we may think, "Poor thing, I guess he can't help it, but what a bore he is!" Or again, as concerns another minster's wife, "Why does she dress like that? Out of the missionary barrel, no doubt!" Or as a prominent women's club member looms up before us, we may think: "She probably won't even see me; she's so stuck up."

Very natural is all such drifting of the mind, but it is completely out of line with God's law of love. We do not need to atone by rushing up and embracing the minister's wife, which would probably embarrass her, nor do we need to run after the graceless boys and instruct them in good manners, even if we can catch them for a moment when their motorcycles are not roaring. ". . . Whatsoever things are true, . . . honest, . . . just, . . . pure, . . . lovely, . . . of good report, . . . think on these things" (Phil 4:8).

This is the first thing I had to master when learning the law of faith. It helped me to remind myself of it every night when I went to bed and every morning when I arose, praying for grace to make this change in my thinking, and giving thanks that my prayer was being answered and that I was going to learn to like everybody, to fear nothing, to despise no one.

Perhaps you are fearing that this change in your thinking toward the town and the people in it will be very difficult. It need not be so! Just play it lightly, like a game. Make in your mind a picture of your town as a place of light and joy. Imagine God's light shining into it so that people will from time to time look up to see if the sun has come through the clouds, but at that time it will not be the sun at all. It will be a mysterious radiance that seems to disappear when one tries to look directly at it, and yet does not really disappear, but surrounds all things with gentleness. In this light you will see beauty where you never before noticed it—an ugly old house transformed into quaintness, a tiny garden suddenly become a bit of shining loveliness, faces of people softened with wistful gentleness, trees by the roadside shining as though with inner light. Are you then seeing things that are not so? On the contrary; you are seeing that which is so, but which up to now you have been unable to see!

Some people feel called to go forth into a town or into the wider world and win people to Jesus, and very likely they are so called. They are evangelists. My own parents were evangelists who went to China in order to convert the heathen. They did it too, and I know that the Lord is rewarding them even now in heaven. For years I felt a bit guilty about the fact that I myself cannot do that. There is a certain shyness in me that simply freezes up my mind when I try to "win people for Jesus." Yet I have led many people to Jesus, not by testifying about Him, but by doing His works in my own small way: praying for the sick so that they are healed, and setting free in His name those who are bound by darkness or the chains of depression. As a matter of fact, this is the way that Jesus showed people the love of God, by healing the sick and setting free those chained in the depths of their own minds. He did not even tell His disciples who He was, and we remember the message that He sent to John the Baptist, who had sent an inquiry as to whether He was the Christ. He said, "Go your way, and tell John what things ye have seen and heard; how that the blind see, the lame walk, the lepers are cleansed, the deaf hear, the dead are raised, to the poor the gospel is preached" (Luke 7:22).

If not all of us are called to be evangelists, like my missionary parents, that is fine, and if you shrink from speaking forth holy things, do not despair. We are called to do different things in different ways; you can win people to Jesus and create a feeling of His love in those with whom you come in contact without saying a word, if you can pray with enough faith to release His light. Those with whom you come in contact, I say. If you want to release God's light in the place where you live, then it is a great help if you do come in contact with your fellow-townsmen, taking part in some of their activities, sharing some of their interests and amusements. In the New Jersey town where my husband was rector, I took part in the things that interested me, and he wisely encouraged me to do so. Having studied drama, and having always been interested in plays, I joined the Players' Club and from time to time delighted my soul (for I am a born ham) by directing and acting in harmless amateur plays. I even wrote some! Also I accepted invitations to parties and played innocent games of cards, but never, I assure you, for money. My Presbyterian ancestors would have turned over in their graves! Then of course there were ladies' teas and luncheons and an occasional dinner party. All these things were good. How can you let your light shine if there is no one to see it shining? Many of my more socially acceptable friends pretended to know nothing about my prayer interest, but if a husband or a child became ill, they would call on me, secretly, like Nicodemus. So the light shone even in darkness, as it did in Jesus' time.

So pray for your home, and your town, and your garden. These are not "musts," you understand. They are only suggestions, as when children play together one suggests a particular game and everyone responds, "That'll be fun!" I have spoken of praying for gardens already, but I love to come back to it; you might say that this whole book is variations on a theme, the theme of praying for God's earth—and greatly enjoying it!

You do not need to say a formal prayer as you go out in early spring to see whether your daffodils are coming up, but when you do see the little green shoots poking through the ground, you need not fear to say, "Oh, thank you, Lord! Oh, Lord, bless them! Thank you, Lord!" And you needn't be afraid to talk directly to the daffodils, if you like, and say, "Oh, aren't you wonderful to come pushing up through all that snow (if you live in a snowy climate!). Oh, thank you! I love you!" Now, this manner of speech is possibly not one to announce to the town; it is between you, your flowers, and their Creator. But let no one who may come across you in earnest conversation with your flowers think you silly. You are not silly at all. You are merely living in God's light, and rejoicing in God's life, and being part of His creation.

And do the flowers really grow better? Of course they do. God's light like a fountain, gushes forth, pulsing out of Him. This is life! "Man shall not live by bread alone, but by every word that proceedeth out of the mouth of God" (Matt. 4:4). Our words go forth upon our breath, and they go forth in a certain rhythm. So, we can easily imagine, do the words of God; He is speaking forth to us on a current of the breath of life. In this life is light, and the light is the life of men. It is by the continuing and recurrent breathing forth of the life of God that we live. He is the fountain of life, the original source of the light, and by His will His Son Jesus Christ, our Lord, brought that life into this planet and commissioned us to continue to conduct it in our small wavelengths into the world around us. That means, I am sure, both the sentient world and the part of the creation which has, as we say, no capacity to feel, and yet I know that it does feel, in ways far beyond the reach of our senses. When I talk to my flowers they seem to talk back to me, or at least to give back to me the same kind of light and love of God that I am giving them.

At our rectory, people used to say to me, "Your flowers are wonderful! How can you get such lovely blossoms in this tiny space tucked in here behind the parish house with so little sun? How do you do it?"

I don't really grow my own garden, but God does, supplying with the sunlight of His love the lack of sun in shadowy places, just as He can do in our lives. Remember Sidney Lanier's poem, quoted in chapter 2?

But the olives they were not blind to him,
The little gray leaves were kind to him,
The thorn tree had a mind to him,
When into the woods he came.

I wonder if they are still there, and if they still remember Him, those ancient olive trees in Gethsemane. Probably not. Too many tourists may have filled the place with talk and smoke—unless maybe they have so filled it with their loving prayers that one does not notice anything else.

Yes, do send God's light into your flower garden, and it will give back a measure of that light and life to you! And if you have no flower garden, but only a potted plant on your window sill, then at times go forth out of your small quarters and find the beauty of the world around you in other people's gardens, and in parks, and in the countryside beyond your town. Something in us longs for the stillness and beauty of the trees, shining in the sun or stark and wistful against a winter sky. So often we think that we would like to go way out into the country, and wander beside a little stream, and see if the wild violets are in bloom. And then we say to ourselves, "No, the kitchen floor needs to be scrubbed," or, "I can't leave the children," or "I must get these accounts in order."

I say to you that the kitchen floor does not need cleaning nearly as much as your tired mind needs to be scrubbed clean of all the worry about floors and sinks and ironing! And *don't* leave the children; take them with you! They will love it! Once in early spring I took my three small children with me into a bit of woods that I knew. We parked in dry grass just off a dirt road, and I dropped my key, which most reprehensibly was not on a chain. A brass key among long dry yellow grass! "Oh, Lord, help me find it!" I prayed, and I went forward. I did not see it; how could one see down into the dry grass? But my toe touched something, and I looked down and there was the key! Apparently the Lord was not annoyed with me for leaving piles of laundry sprinkled in my back kitchen. Apparently He knew, as I did, that it was more important to take the children into the woods to see the wild lupines! There they were, masses of them, blue amid the somber green of the pine trees. I have never forgotten it, and I don't think the children have either. The lupines did not speak in words, but they spoke in the speech of beauty, and so they comforted and strengthened us. The invisible radiance of God's light illumines the lonely places within us, and tells us of His love.

"All thy works shall praise thee, O Lord; and thy saints shall bless thee" (Ps. 145:10).

But surely we should turn away from this world and keep our minds on heaven—or so some pious people used to tell me in my youth. Oh, I don't think so! If God loved this world enough to send His only begotten Son into it (John 3:16), then surely we also can love this world. God did not send His Son to condemn the world, as that passage continues, "but that the world through him might be saved" (v. 17).

His creation is the world that came into being through His breathing forth of the breath of life; it is the garden of this world planted by His love. He is delighted when He sees the many ways in which we have made the world more beautiful! It pleases Him to look upon our California freeways planted with bright African daisies and oleander shining in the sunlight! He rejoices in lovely parks, with flamingoes stealing with their long rosy legs through still waters, or peacocks screaming their wild delight. Our mountains please Him, all shining in the sun, their snow-capped peaks soaring into the heavens. His people please Him when they create upon this earth gardens and tall buildings and pleasant homes filled with love. It is a joy to the Creator to feel His love pulsing through time, through galaxies in the far heavens and stars unkown and without number. It delights Him to see His little creatures here below exploring His mysteries and finding the hidden treasures of earth and sea. Someone said rather quaintly that he could just imagine God making a pearl, hiding it in an oyster, and saying, "There, I wonder if man will find *that!*"

The seas that enfold this earth are also of Him. Even more than the beauties of flowers and mountains does the sea conduct to us God's light. I mean this quite literally and return often to this truth for my comfort; water is a natural conductor of God's light, and the illimitable vistas of the ocean speak to us of God if we but make their acquaintance and listen to them. "They that go down to the sea in ships, that do business in great waters" (Ps. 107:23) have always felt the fascination of the sea. What draws us to the ocean is more than its beauty and the swing of its constant movement. It is the light, God's invisible light of so high an intensity and so fine a wavelength that we cannot see it with our eyes, which flows into us as we rest beside the sea, or sail upon it, or travel in great ships across its vastness. We can abide speechless for hours and let it talk to us, only attuning our spirits so that we can be at one with its vast glory—sun glinting on the towering waves, and sea birds soaring over them, winds carrying their spray and tossing it far away, and wavelets coming up to our feet, touching us with cold fingers and drawing back again along wet sand into the thundering depths of another wave.

What has all this to do with God? Everything! I always feel like laughing when, from the Episcopal prayer book, I sing about whales blessing the Lord, along with all other creatures that move in the waters; yet it is joyous laughter, for I know that there is meaning and great truth therein. God's life created and supports all living creatures, and in some dim way they feel that life and rejoice in it.

If even whales can praise Him, so can I! And I can let His light shine through me into the town where I live, blessing and praising Him that the knowledge of His love will increase there more and more. And I can pray for the blessing of His prosperity upon my city, and upon my house, and upon my business or my husband's business, for we can pray with faith for the health of a business just as we can for bodily health.

Prayer for whatever contributes to our prosperity and family well-being is an easy prayer to pray, and the whole Bible is full of it. Look up prosperity and related words in a concordance and you will see what I mean. Yet in spite of this clear teaching that God is the source of all that we need, and that He will neither fail nor forsake us, many Christians fear that it is wrong to pray about money. They have grim ideas about "filthy lucre." Well, money does not have to be filthy! If it is honestly earned and wisely and generously used, it ought to shine with the light of God's righteousness. It can, and it will, if we bless our cash, houses, bank accounts, investments and the businesses that support them.

When any material need arises we should not hesitate to pray the prayer of faith concerning it. Some Christians fail to do this because they say that Jesus was poor and He had nowhere to lay His head. That is true. Jesus gave up having His own home so that He could go out into the world and do the great work of redemption given Him by the Father, which He chose to do, because He and the Father are one. He had no place to lay His head because He was out on the road preaching and doing miracles. Our dear Lord must have been very tired when He said, "The foxes have holes, and the birds of the air have nests; but the Son of man hath not where to lay his head" (Matt. 8:20). How we love Him for it! He could have been in any one of the heavenly mansions that He would choose, yet here He was wandering around a stony land, night coming down, and He not knowing where He might find a place to rest. This was not because He could not pay His way at an inn. He was neither poor nor destitute. He wore a seamless robe, no doubt woven by hand, which was so valuable that the soldiers cast lots for it after He was crucified. Soldiers would not wear such a robe, but they knew that they could sell it for a great sum.

Furthermore, if Jesus was ever short of cash, all heaven and earth were His from which to draw. Once when He did not at the moment have on Him the coin required for the temple tax, He sent Peter to find it in a fish's mouth (Matt. 17:27)! I suppose the fish had found it on the bottom of the lake and could not swallow it. Jesus could see the horizon, and beyond the horizon, and through all time when He needed to, so He probably said, "Father, I need a shekel," and saw it, and sent for it.

So we can say in a time of need, "Father, I need five dollars," or fifty, or five hundred, or indeed five thousand and it will come to us, or we will find it somehow, if we believe, just as health will come to us, or we will find it, if we believe.

When money does come to us in response to our prayer, of course we will want to give a part of it to the Lord. We are told in the Old Testament just how much to give—in the beginning. Later we can give far more! The least we are to give is a tenth, or tithe, as it is called in the Bible.

Now if we really need money badly, and if we have prayed, and still the money does not come, why would that be? Probably we have not opened a door for it in our minds by *believing* that it will come. The principle is exactly the same as in healing. First we say, "Oh, Lord, please make me well!" and then we must set ourselves to believing it will be so. We imagine it; we see a picture of it in our minds; we give thanks for it. That is the greatest thing of all. Prayer is not much use unless we thank God for giving us the health, or the money, or whatever it is that we are praying for.

So when we pray for prosperity, let us give thanks for the blessings that are coming from God. Let us imagine the business in which we work, or from which our money comes, and see it thriving and doing a good, useful job, seeing by faith the moneys that it needs pouring in and out of it in all good ways. We do not need to dream up those ways. In fact it is best if we do not, but just leave the means in God's hands and give thanks. In fact, we can leave all our money in God's loving care, and know that He will take charge of it and supply our every need.

All of this I taught in the early days to a daily vacation Bible school. On the last day of the school my son, then about eight years old, went home from the parish house and met his father who said, "Jack, you have earned all you owed for those windows you broke except twenty-eight cents. So I'm going to give you that twenty-eight cents, and I don't want you breaking any more windows, do you hear?"

Jack joyfully pocketed the money and said, "Hot dog! I prayed for that at vacation school!"

Well, why not? Full payment for broken windows was a very big project for a small boy. Some of us have bigger ones, and if they reflect real needs of a home or business honestly conducted, we can pray with faith, that is, expecting to receive what we have needed. Unless we have the faith, it is not too likely to come to us. If we do have the faith, nothing can stop it from coming to us.

My own experiences are not in the line of business so much as in simple, homely needs, but I will tell you a true story to build your faith. Once I was visiting a friend and we were going marketing together. She changed her shoes just before leaving the house, and then changed her pocketbook to match her shoes. Off we went with the money that her husband had given her, twenty one dollar bills, neatly bound with a strip of brown paper, carefully placed in her pocketbook. While we were in the market I noticed that my friend's purse was hanging open, and the money was gone. Of course we searched the store, even looking under counters in case the money had been carelessly kicked aside, and we inquired at the desk, quite uselessly. I had enough money with me for our immediate needs. But I said to my friend: "That is your money, rightfully earned by your husband and given to you. It is yours; therefore you have a perfect right to pray for it and give thanks for it, knowing that it will come back to you. Of course," I added, weakening slightly, "it may not come back to you in quite the same form. Perhaps it will come in the mail; someone might remember an old debt, or send you a gift. But just give thanks, because it is yours by divine right, and it is bound to come to you."

So we gave thanks all the way home. She then went upstairs, and there in the middle of her bed was that same packet of twenty one dollar bills! She did not tell her husband then, for it would have been asking too much of any husband to believe such a story. He, like some others, might have said, "Oh, you just forgot it. It was on your bed all the time. You left it there." But she didn't, for I had seen her put it into the purse that she took to the grocery store.

How did God give it back to her? I don't know. I only have to believe, and give thanks!

CHAPTER 7

"For God so loved the world, that he gave his only begotten Son, that whosoever believeth in him should not perish, but have everlasting life" (John 3:16).

We are very familiar with this verse, which I have already quoted. Have we ever noticed that it does not say, "God so loved man," or "God so loved mankind"? We are apt to think that He created the world for us, so that we would have a place to live. Can it be possible that in fact He created people for the world, because He so loved the world? The world, as we have already noted, is much greater than this planet earth. The world contains suns beyond suns, myriads of planets rotating around them, even galaxies beyond galaxies. The world has unknown numbers of galaxies or star-groups. Did St. John really mean the world to be the universe, that is, all created things, when he wrote that verse? Whatever his idea of the universe might have been, God knew how great a thing he was saying even if St. John did not. The Bible says that it was because God so loved the world—the work of His hands or of His holy imagination—that He sent His Son to die for the sins of the little people on one planet, the earth, so that these people might become the sons of God and take care of the earth that He put in their charge. I have already quoted some of the parables of Jesus that illustrate this truth, that we are here at least to take care of *this* earth, and no one knows how far our prayers can reach into the universe.

We are told that God loves this creation of His, and we know very well, many of us do, that it is possible for us to love earth and trees, grass and flowers, particularly if they are our own.

Years ago my husband and I bought a little run-down farm in New England. The old house was about to slide down the hill, for the foundations of rough stones were bulging in the damp, dirt-floored cellar. Everything about the house had to be rebuilt or strengthened, and my husband did the work with enthusiasm. The grounds were rough and neglected, and I made them beautiful, planting flowers in every possible corner, and pruning old raspberry vines and lilac bushes, that they might bring forth more fruit or flowers. We loved it! The feeling we had for that place was more than mere admiration and joy; it was *love*. After my husband died and I eventually moved to California, it seemed best to sell the old place in the East, for I could not traipse across the whole country to look after it.

When I left that blissful summer paradise full of wistful memories, I stood and took one last look at the peaceful meadows shining in the sun, and it seemed to me that they were in mourning. This may have been my imagination, but one thing is sure: I so loved the earth of that place that I can understand how the Creator can actually love this little earth. It seems as though He did, and sent His Son Jesus to redeem it from our sins. Our usual concept is that He came to redeem us from our sins so that we can go to heaven. But can it be that He had a wider concept and plan for salvation, not just of the earth, but of the world? Can it be that the sacrifice of Jesus was not only for us living now, but for all people through all eternity, so that the loving purpose for which He created all worlds might be fulfilled? You may think this a great project, and so it is. But it is not impossible that we can help God to fulfill His purposes in all the world, as in fact He has commanded us to do. We do this in a general way every time we pray the Lord's prayer, but just as we pray for our own special needs in addition to praying this overall prayer, so we can pray for our special bits of earth in addition to the all-encompassing, "Thy kingdom come." When we ask a special blessing, as I have already discussed doing, on our own homes and yards, and on the streets in front of the yards, the towns or cities in which we live, our schools, what do we really mean? Why, we are praying that God will pour out His light and life on that place or in that house.

In Australia a few years ago I prayed for a young woman in deep depression. She felt that evil forces were attacking her and her children. The children were afraid to go to bed at night, and sometimes awoke screaming with terror. I do not claim to understand all this matter, but I prayed that any evil force that might be in her would be cast out, and that God would bless her house, filling every room and every closet, even the hallways, with His presence, an invisible light, a palpable peace. The next evening she again came to church, looking like an entirely different person—beautiful, peaceful, and about ten years younger. She said that overnight the atmosphere in her house had changed. (The atmosphere of a place means more than the air. It means the whole feeling of the place. When it is changed, the very rate of the vibrations is changed to peace from agitation, as in this case. This is a *physical* change.) The woman said that she no longer felt cold and depressed but light and happy when entering her house, and her children had slept peacefully all night.

Our homes may not be infested with evil, as that young woman's home had been, but we would still do well to ask God daily to renew His blessings in our home, filling it more and more with His light, and extending His blessing to the yard or garden, so that there also, a life beyond the life that we see may increase and shine. Most of us cannot see that light, but some very perceptive people actually can see it, like the boy mentioned previously who said he always saw sort of a shining cloud around my house. Many people can sense, even if they do not see anything, the feeling of a house where God's light abides. Sometimes this feeling extends to a whole town, and people coming to it say it is a peaceful place, perhaps not knowing that God's peace has been called for, and has settled there. In such a town the crime rate decreases, naturally. Satan has a hard time abiding in the light of God's love. In such a town industry improves and crops are more abundant. Everything prospers, naturally! God is a God of abundance and prosperity, not of poverty and want.

In speaking of my summer home in New England, I stated that I loved the place. I had toward it not only an impersonal liking but that sense of deep, personal tenderness that we call love. Why? There are other fields and woods quite as lovely, and many places more beautiful. But to that place I had given something of myself. The fields and woodlands were permeated with a sense of tenderness that had come from me and my husband. Therefore I loved it with a very special love.

So it is that God loves the world. He has given it something of himself; He has created it from the love and the power and the beauty of His own being. There is an essence of God's light in the very earth on which we live.

He is our Father. We do not look like Him, for He lives not in a body that can be seen, but certain of the traits that are in Him have been passed on to us. I do not look like my mother, but I have inherited, for instance, her love of beauty. She could see beauty even in a dying leaf in the fall of the year; so can I.

We do not look like God. That would be impossible, for He is not of flesh and blood. He is a light too intense for our human eyes to see Him. Moses longed to see Him, but the Lord told him that no one could see Him and live. However, the Lord said to Moses: "And it shall come to pass, while my glory passeth by, that I will put thee in a cleft of the rock, and will cover thee with my hand while I pass by: and I will take away mine hand, and thou shalt see my back parts: but my face shall not be seen" (Exod. 33:22-23). So Moses was permitted to see only a small, veiled shining of a light too great for human eyes to see. We inherit only a small, an infinitesimal, portion of this light, passed on to us through Jesus Christ, who is our light. In very simple words, we do not look like God, but we are like Him in our small way when we live close enough to His Son Jesus. Then a ray of God's light can shine through us and illumine the place where we stand, the bit of earth that is ours, and shine forth into the world around us.

That being the case, why can't we just pray for God to bless the whole world, and leave it at that? We can, and we do, but our light is not great enough to encompass the whole world, and so we need to pray also in smaller and more particularized ways.

Let me use an analogy in order to make this clear. God is the source, the center of light that is also life, and that erupts forth from Him like a fountain. "For with thee is the fountain of life" (Ps. 36:9), remember? From this life all life was created and evolved into suns with their attendant planets, and moons, and into the living beings that live upon our earth, and possibly on other earths as well.

Upon this earth, at least, the human beings lost their awareness of God and of His goodness, and of our need to preserve that goodness so that His light could shine within us for our health and comfort, and through us into the world. God's spiritual light "infinite, eternal, and invisible" according to the Presbyterian Shorter Catechism, could not reach through to us who are encased in flesh. We needed someone to transform that light into a milder intensity and a smaller wavelength so that we could absorb it. It is like electricity which is everywhere, in the air and in the earth, but is not available for our use. Occasionally when the air is very highly charged, an electric spark will crackle from our garments when we move, but this is useless to us.

However, men of science have invented the powerhouse, which catches this same flow of an intangible power and an invisible vibration of light, and steps it down to a current that can furnish light, heat and power in forms usable by us.

Jesus is our Transformer. In Him is the mysterious union of divinity and humanity. The power of God entered into a pure virgin and caused her to conceive a Son, who was both divine and human. The virgin Mary was betrothed to Joseph, a young man whom we greatly honor for his faithfulness. He and Mary were properly married but were not living together as man and wife. I have been told that this was according to the eastern custom by which bride and groom went on their honeymoon accompanied by a number of uncles, aunts and cousins. This gave them an opportunity to know each other, for mates were chosen by the parents, as in old China, and the bride and groom (aged about twelve and fourteen respectively) had very likely never seen each other until the marriage ceremony. I do not know at what point they "came together" in China, but a wise elder usually told them the right time, or the "lucky day," as the Chinese would have said.

Before they came together Joseph discovered that Mary was already with child. Whose child? God's child, His very Son, the inheritor of His power and glory, living inconceivably yet truly in the baby of a woman. After this child was grown, and had lived among men for years, and taught them of God's goodness, and healed them by God's power, He then immersed himself in them by entering into the very depths of their suffering, and by rising triumphantly out of death into a new life. Thus Jesus opened the door, that men could rise with Him.

The above is a very brief summary of what I have endeavored to expound in *Behold Your God*, and even more intimately in *Twice Seven Words*.

Thus it is that through the Transformer, Jesus, the light enters into us. We are, as we have already noted, like the little light bulbs that illumine our houses. One bulb can at the very most illumine one room. There would be no use in saying, "Why can't I just turn on the living room lamp and have enough light to fill the house and the yard and my neighbor's houses?" No use; it does not work that way!

So when we say, "Let there be light over the whole world," or, "Thy kingdom come," that is the statement of a wish, but we need to implement that statement. We need ourselves to become conductors of the light—lamps, light bulbs, through which the light can shine and illumine our bit of the world, our homes, our schools, our places of business. We have spoken of praying for our local school, or for one classroom in it, and imagining God's light increasing therein. His light is also love because He is also love, and as it increases in a room, it begins to feel warm and cozy and safe. One teacher told me of a child who came back after recess and sank down into her seat with a sigh of relief, and said, "Oh, it's good to get back here!" In that schoolroom the teacher was a conductor of the light, and therefore it had become a place of peace.

When God's kingdom has come in our homes, let us go one step further and pray the prayer of faith that His kingdom may come in our place of business or, if it is a housewife who is praying, the husband's place of business. This is, as we have already indicated, a great adventure! God is a worker. He is interested in any honest industry. "My Father worketh hitherto, and I work," said Jesus (John 5:17). Man is by nature a worker, and he is commanded to work not only for the sake of the job, but also for the sake of his own soul. Since we are the children of God, we have inherited His passionate creativity. Therefore it is completely in line with His laws that we should ask His blessing on our work, asking His light and energy to be in it, working toward prosperity and peace. God's light can shine into any place of honest business—office or tool shop, farm or dairy, filling station or department store, and even a building site, full of roaring bulldozers though it may be. Any business that is blessed of the Lord will bring forth abundantly, to the comfort of many people.

Now, the prayer that *works* is the prayer of faith. Therefore, after asking for God's light to shine in the place of business, stepping up its production, one should give thanks that this is being done, visualizing (seeing by faith) the place filled with peace and prosperity, and thanking God for it.

If business seems to you an unworthy object to pray about, read the Bible! Read especially the Old Testament. Abraham, Isaac, Jacob and all the rest of them asked God to bless their fields and crops, and they prospered exceedingly because they trusted God.

We have made for ourselves a theory that God's love and life are only for people, and that even animals, let alone plants, are beneath His notice. That is not true!

For instance, Edith Drury and I were once at Lee Abbey, a wonderful Christian retreat center combined with a farm on the beautiful coast of Devon in England. One afternoon Edith walked down to the shore and returned through the steep, green cow pastures where Ben, a very serious young Christian, stopped his tractor and called to her. "Edith," he said, "I know that Agnes is very busy, but would you have time to pray a healing of the memories prayer for Sheila? She is very nervous and seems to be getting upset, and I'm sure it would help her." Edith agreed gladly, and inquired what would be a convenient time for Sheila, assuming that she was Ben's fiancee. He said that he thought that after tea would be just fine, and so Edith went to the workmen's outdoor tea, ate slabs of bread with Marmite on it, and drank very black tea. "Now," she said to Ben, "where will I find Sheila?"

"In the cow stable, naturally," he replied.

Sheila was a cow.

Edith therefore followed Ben into the cow stable which was

112

rather mucky, she said, with cows standing in long rows waiting to be milked. Bill, another cowhand, was busy with his milking. "Oh, I say, Bill," said Ben, "Edith has come to give Sheila the laying on of hands. Would you care to join us?"

"Oh, no, no!" cried Bill, a bit wide-eyed. "You carry on!"

So Edith, introduced to Sheila, which to her looked like all the others, laid hands upon her back (the least sticky area she could see!), Ben joining her from Sheila's other side. She prayed that the love and light of God would go all the way back through Sheila's heifer-hood, healing all traumatic experiences, remembered or not, in her subconscious, and make her a happy, cream-filled Christian cow, certainly with no more tendencies to kick and be nervous.

It worked! Ben reported that after the prayer Sheila was a transformed cow. She was serene and friendly, followed Ben around, and no longer kicked when being milked.

I could fill the rest of this chapter, and indeed most of the book, with such incidents. For instance, there was a young veterinary doctor who loved and prayed for his "patients" and who prospered exceedingly, for even the most seriously injured or sick animals in his care seemed to recover. There was a big businessman, very wealthy, who gathered the heads of departments together when his factory opened each morning, and prayed with them for the day's work. There is an artistically inclined woman who asks God to bless her pastels, and who has become professional, painting on commission and being well paid for her pictures, even though her main work has been something quite different. (That woman is myself.)

Of course God can bless the work of our hands and of our minds, for He himself is a Creator, and as He blesses our work with prosperity it is also blessed with love, for God is love. Those words, "God is love" (1 John 4:8), are probably the first words of scripture many of us ever heard.

A question arises: Shall we make this practice of praying for our work public knowledge? My own feeling is that very often God's power works better when protected by secrecy, though perhaps not always. There is a time to testify and a time to be silent. Should we, for instance, put a picture of Jesus in our office? In some cases that might help to create the feeling of His presence there, but in other cases it might be inappropriate. I do not feel that we should be under any compulsion to advertise our faith that way. If we really believe in Jesus, people will know it.

You might also go a step further than praying for your own business or one in which you are involved, and pray for a big business, one that stretches from continent to continent. I believe that the future of the earth depends as much, or more, on the big businesses that span the globe as it does on governments. Any business that is dedicated to the Lord can have tremendous repercussions on this earth. I cannot speak from experience here, but I have heard of a very great business that became dedicated to the Lord because its head was a real Christian, filled with the Spirit, and with the love of the Lord. He won others to his beliefs, and his business conferences began with prayer. No one was hired except with prayer, and no one was fired except with prayer plus an honest, kind talk explaining the reasons and giving suggestions for the future. Needless to say, that business grew and expanded, with branches set up in foreign countries, all prospering. One cannot calculate its influence.

Of such is the kingdom of heaven made!

CHAPTER 8

We have considered how to build up the light-energy of God in homes, schools, businesses and, in a general way, in churches. The church is indeed one place where this light of God should, and can, shine even more brightly than anywhere else. A church can become in truth *holy*, so that out of it healing can go forth into the world.

The very presence of God abides in a church, just as He abode in Old Testament times in the temple, and even in the tabernacle in the wilderness. The latter was a tent, to be moved as the people moved, yet it was gloriously appointed with purple and fine linen and candlesticks of gold, and its priests' robes were hung with bells and pomegranates. All this was to make a fit place for the glory of God to inhabit, and so great was that light, so real was that power, that the ark within which the holy objects were kept was, we would say, radioactive with a holy energy.

How much more should our churches of today be filled with energy when Jesus Christ has come to abide in them! Our churches do not need bells and pomegranates, nor cloth of gold, nor fine-twined linen. Some churches are built to show forth in their very bricks and mortar the glory of God, and others are simply plain meeting houses for the people of God. The important thing is that in any church the light of Christ can shine to the comfort of His people and to the illumination of at least a bit of the world. It all depends on the faith of the people who worship there.

Long ago in New Zealand a young man came to the minister of the Presbyterian church where I was holding a mission and said to him, "What's been going on here? I just passed the church and so much power, or something, came out of it that I almost fell down on the pavement."

The minister told him that we had been having a healing mission. "So that's it!" responded the young man, quite satisfied. He understood. Something was happening in that church, so of course there was power.

Something is supposed to happen wherever Christian people gather together to worship God. The Episcopal prayer book is full of prayers for the earth, the family of nations, those who are sick or afflicted. In other churches prayers for these concerns may not be written down in a book, but petitions for healing, peace, etc., are apt to be included in the minister's pastoral prayer. However, let us be honest; we do not very often hear of miracles taking place through these general prayers. People do not expect miracles to happen, and therefore they do not happen: God's power remains static. The world is full of His energy. By His word the worlds were made. By the crucifixion and resurrection of Jesus Christ the power of the enemy was broken, and by the action of the Holy Spirit the miraculous energy of Jesus himself is brought into this world for our use and comfort.

Then why do not miracles happen whenever Christian people are gathered together? You who read, I who write, we ordinary Christians, have the answer to that because we are the answer. There is no magic in the church building itself, in spite of all its stained-glass windows and candles. They are only symbols of the reality; *we* are to be the candles of the Lord, and *we* the glowing windows through whom His glory shines forth. The light in the church must shine through us the people, the congregation.

Now I will suggest to you a really wonderful venture that you can undertake all by yourself, telling no one unless you have some good prayer partners who would like to join you in it. When you go to church, offer yourself to God as a channel for His light. His light must have a channel, just as the light of electric power must have a fixture through which to shine. Wipe off the dust from this fixture of your soul; remove from your inner being any dust of old resentments that you can remember; and ask God to bring to your mind any evil or fearful thought that might interfere with the clear shining of His light. God is love, and His light shines on the thoughtwaves of love.

One time a man came to me after church and said, "Did you pray for me in church?"

"No," I said truthfully, "I didn't."

"Well, someone must have," he said. "I felt just terrible when I came to church, all cross and worried and depressed. I didn't want to come, but my wife made me. Then all of a sudden everything cleared up, and I felt wonderful!"

"Naturally!" I said. "Someone must have been praying for you." Naturally!

Once on a weekday a man went to my husband's study and asked to talk with him. Ted was busy at the moment and told the man to go into the church and wait for him. He would come in a few minutes. In twenty minutes Ted went into the church in search of him. He was not there. A bit disturbed, Ted even looked under the pews, in case he had somehow come to grief, but there was no sign of him. A year later Ted received a letter from someone he did not know in a distant state.

117

"You will not remember me," the letter said, "but a year ago on this date I came to your study to see you. I had been in depression for a long time, and somehow felt that I would find help through you. You were occupied, and told me to go into the church and wait for you. I sat in a pew, and a sort of peace began coming into me. The longer I sat there, the better I felt, and I finally realized that I didn't need to talk to you at all. I went out of the church perfectly well. Thank you for having a church like that!"

Every church should, and can, be like that. I have mentioned the church in New Zealand where I was holding a healing mission, and the man passing on the street who came in to ask, "What is happening to this church?" The fact is that healing was happening in that church, and where the works of God are done, there God abides.

Jesus showed forth the glory of God by healing those who came to Him. That is the first and simplest way that I know of to glorify our Creator, because healing is the continuing of His creative power.

Many churches hope and pray that this power will go forth from them, but I want to make a few comments on why it may not always happen. The most common way that churches pray for the sick or troubled people, according to my experience, is by reading a long list of names, beginning, "Our prayers are requested for . . ." or something like that. Now there is no harm in this; it is a friendly gesture, but I cannot feel any power in it, nor can I really pray for these people. There is not time. For my prayer to be effective I need to concentrate all my energies of prayer and faith on one person, imagine that person well, hold him up into the light of God, and see by faith His power shining in while I give thanks that he now is becoming well. I cannot do this while the minister is reading off a lot of other names. There may be other values in the reading of such a list. It shows goodwill toward these people, and it may suggest to someone in the congregation a person for whom to pray the prayer of faith on returning home. But certainly and surely the reading of a list does not evoke in the church the power that heals and shines forth into the world. Just think, if the reading or reciting of a list of names were sufficient to bring healing, our Lord Jesus could have stayed quietly at home in the carpenter shop and just read off lists. That way he would not have gotten into trouble.

In the reading of a list the assumption is that we are merely asking God to heal someone. There is no harm in that, of course, but it is far more effective if we realize that God heals by the light of Jesus Christ shining through us, through people, just as the light of electricity, all-pervasive as it is, does not light our houses unless they are wired and connected to the powerhouse. So prayer does not enlighten the world unless we are connected with the powerhouse, Jesus Christ, and unless we ourselves function as light bulbs, His energy shining through us. If all Christians in a church service were to do this kind of praying, each choosing one person and not trying to encompass a whole list, then the light of God would not only go forth to that individual in need but would overflow into the church itself, making it indeed a healing church.

"What is that light around the cross?" people often asked my husband. "Do you have some unusual kind of lighting fixture there?"

"There is no lighting fixture for the cross," he would reply.

"But I saw a light. . . ."

He would reply, "Many people see that light."

What was that light? It was the actual energy of God, available and in motion. Why then is it not seen in every church, and why does not the power of that light go forth to do miracles upon the land? Let's face the fact that the power does not usually so go forth. Does everyone on the prayer list leap out of bed and rejoice in health? You know that they do not. Why? Because those who pray for them do not expect them to leap up and be well; it is as simple as that! What we can do about it is to forget the list, and simply pray for God's light to shine in that church so powerfully that miracles will happen there.

Once a woman was driving past my husband's church on her way to Atlantic City, where she intended to drown herself in the ocean. It was Good Friday, though that meant nothing to her, but as she drove past she noticed the church and had an impulse to stop and go inside. The three-hour service was just beginning, and she intended to stay just a few minutes and then slip out, but she began to feel better and better, and ended by staying the whole three hours. At the door on her way out she told my husband how she had received perfect healing during the service, and now was well, no longer depressed or even thinking of destroying herself. "Thank you for having a church like this!" she said, using the same words he had heard from that man who came for counseling but left, healed, without ever speaking with my husband.

It is the congregation that can fill a church with such power. No minister can do it alone. So I appeal to you members of the congregations in uncounted churches to begin with one person—yourself! Before you go to church, prepare for the service by forgiving and being forgiven, that is, learning to like any person whom you have not liked, and asking God to forgive you for any wrong that you have done. When you get to church, make sure that this is accomplished by looking about the congregation and seeing whether anyone's face makes you feel uncomfortable. If so, pray for the love of God to enter into that person, healing any old hurts or sorrows that make the face unpleasant to you, and to fill him or her with His joy. Then choose maybe one other person in the congregation who needs healing, and pray for him or her to be healed, giving thanks for the healing that is coming. As you do this in your church at every service, you will find your church more and more filled with God's light and power.

Some of you reading this will think with sorrow that to follow these suggestions will be impossible for you because you have to teach Sunday school during the church hour. I am sorry that some churches nowadays hold their church school and their main service at the same hour, for it weakens both of them, some of their most valuable members being tied up in the church school. It is also bad for the children, for they need not only instruction in the Bible but also an experience of God's light which they are perfectly able to receive in a church service—often more able than adults, in fact.

Once a little boy about three years old was in church with his parents, sitting quite still as he had been instructed to do in God's house. Being so small he could not see what went on in the chancel until the rector arose into the pulpit in his white robes and very likely, to the small boy, with a light around him. "Mother!" cried the child loud and clear. "Mother! Is that God?" No, it was not God but His faithful servant, clothed in His light.

A friend of mine once walked down the street to see me, bringing her little boy with her. "I want to go to church!" announced the little one, barely more than an infant.

"But this isn't Sunday," protested his mother.

"I know, but I want to go to church just the same."

Very wisely the mother held his small hand and took him into the church and knelt with him in a pew and said a short prayer. When they came out the little boy's eyes were shining. "Well, I'll say Jesus was in there!" he exclaimed.

So we pray for the light of Christ to increase in all these different places—our homes, our schools, our churches, our towns, our places of employment. What next? All this preliminary prayer and clearing of the way will make it easier to pray for our country, the land in which we live. It will increase our faith in praying general prayers for the nation, whether read from a prayer book or prayed spontaneously.

All too often, however, such prayers for nations and lands consist of moaning and complaining and are not at all the prayer of faith. We deplore all the evil things that go on in our country, complain about them, and then ask God to bless us! God cannot bless us when our minds are full of condemnation and fear! Let us compare this with prayers for the healing of the sick, about which I have already said a good deal. If our minds are fastened on every bad symptom, and if we list them all to God and ask Him to heal the sick person even while we go on thinking about symptoms with moans and complaints, God cannot heal through us. We ourselves are standing in our friend's way by seeing all his bad symptoms. By seeing and deploring them we actually make them worse, for what a person sees in his mind tends to become true. In all my books on healing I have brought forth this point: the mind itself has creative ability, and tends to create what it sees. Therefore in praying for the healing of ourselves or of someone else, we must first change the picture in our minds. We must picture the body well.

The same holds good in praying for our country—in my case, for the United States of America. I have read many articles pointing out lacks and failures of these United States. There may be value in that kind of writing. It will, one hopes, alert some people to reforms of one kind or another. But there is little value as far as prayer with the expectation of results is concerned. Remember, what we see in our minds tends to become true. The more we fret over crime and violence, the more crime and violence we stimulate by our very attention. Therefore, I am going to think about good things, and rejoice in them! Just as in writing about personal healing, I tell examples of triumphant prayer so that all can rejoice in them and thus increase their own faith, so here I shall tell some little stories that show forth the good, sturdy qualities inherent in our great country in order that we all may rejoice in them.

Let us begin in New England. I heard a delightful story about a man who bought a summer home there and went to the local store to purchase paint that he might repaint it. "Yup, yup," said the storekeeper. "I know that house. It'll take four gallons of paint to repaint that house." The outlander went home with his four gallons but returned two weeks later to buy some more.

"You've only finished three sides of that house," said the storekeeper. "And you've used up all that paint? Must have wasted it. Can't see my way clear to selling you any more paint. No, can't see my way clear." And he wouldn't either! He was not going to tolerate wastefulness.

I once strolled down the dirt road and dropped in on my New Hampshire neighbor, Susan, who was out planting tomatoes. "That's a good-looking jacket you've got on, Susan," said I, noting the trim shoulder lines of her khaki jacket.

"My grandfather wore this in the Spanish-American War," she said. And it *was* a good jacket. Why not use it? We in the United States do know what economy is. Some think of us as a great wasteful nation, but that is a one-sided picture. I would rather look at the other side, and rejoice in it, and pray that all of us in all ways will so shepherd our resources.

I was once in Virginia doing some lectures and visiting an old friend in Norfolk. She was engaged in a long telephone conversation, laughing and chatting with much delight. When she finally hung up, I asked, "Who was that you were talking with?"

"Oh, that was Carrie who used to work for me."

I said nothing, for nothing needed to be said, but I was delighted, never before having heard such joyous friendliness between employer and worker. I could tell many more stories, and so could you, illustrating that there is love in our country. We have it in every part of the land, and among all kinds of people. I rejoice in it! I thank God for it! I praise His name for it! And I expect it to be increased more and more, for the more we

123

give God thanks and praise for what we have, the more it will be increased. If on the other hand for some reason that I cannot at all comprehend, we ignore the beauty of the love that can be found among all people of all circumstances, and dwell only on the bits of hate that are also among us, then the love decreases as the hate pushes it away. For the thing on which we fasten our attention tends to become true. That is a law, as unchangeable as the law of the Medes and the Persians.

In Texas, telling churches full of people about the healing love of Jesus Christ, and visiting friends where we were deluged with buckets of shrimp gumbo, pecan pies, fruit cakes and fried chicken, I heard the most beautiful story of love that I have ever heard. A prosperous businessman told me about his mother who, at eighteen, had married a middle-aged widower with eight children. The younger three or four of them came to live with her, and she proceeded to have four or five of her own. After a while her husband disappeared with another woman and left her with eight children and no visible support. They lived in an old gray house down among the bayous, and she worked in the "racket stores," as the five-and-tens were then called. On the way home and in other free time she would sharecrop for some farmers, picking vegetables and keeping some for her family, and she would pick up chips in the woods for fuel. Hers was a desperate struggle for life, and certainly she prayed for help.

One evening just at dark there appeared at the back door a Negro woman and a lad of about fourteen, her grandson. Outside was their mule and wagon. "The Lord told me I'm to come here and live with you, and help you," said the woman.

"But I didn't hire you! I couldn't!" said the lady of the house, thinking the woman must have mistaken the place.

"No, ma'am, I know you didn't. But the Lord told me to come. He said to get the boy to drive me down the river road, and when I saw the house, I'd know it. This is the house; I know it!"

"But I can't pay you," gasped the lady. "I don't have any money, and I've got eight children."

"Yes'm, I know, and I've brought food. I've been getting ready for about a year now. Boy, bring in the tubs of sausage, and the beans, and—"

"But wait!" cried the lady, feeling that all this was as fantastic as a dream. "You can't stay here. I don't have beds, and—"

"I brought my own cot," said Aunt Adeline. "The boy can sleep on the floor tonight, and in the morning he's going back home, and he'll tell my daughter that I found it—the house where the Lord said, 'Stay!' "

"Well, stay 'til the morning," said the lady doubtfully, "and then we'll see." But by morning the boy and the wagon had disappeared.

"I told him to go on home," said Aunt Adeline serenely. "This is where the Lord told me to stay, and I'm staying!"

She did stay for the rest of her life. The man who told me the story remembered how she would sit at the window holding him, the youngest, on her knees, waiting for the mother to come home. Aunt Adeline didn't like cars. She called them "old devils," and when one had a light missing, she would say, "Here comes a one-eyed devil."

The children had only one decent outfit of clothes apiece, so when they got home from school Aunt Adeline made them put on old things while she washed and ironed their school clothes, so that "her" children would "look like folks" when they went to school, she said.

I asked what finally happened to Aunt Adeline, and the answer was that in old age she finally got pneumonia and died. The mother and the children remaining at home nursed her tenderly, to no avail. As a memorial to her the family obtained an old, abandoned two-room cabin and dragged it themselves onto their bit of riverside property. They cleaned and painted it, and found odds and ends of furnishings to make it comfortable, so that it would always be available for any Negro person or couple who had no place to live. When the family had dinner the first servings were always set aside for whomever was in the cabin, and in addition Aunt Adeline's acts of love were continued out into the community by that family and by my friend, the "baby," in particular.

I have told this true and touching story because I love it and rejoice in it, and I want you to rejoice in it also. Thank God for it, and pray, *believing*, that the fountain of love that does abide in this country between races will more and more spring forth to the glory of God and to the bringing in of His kingdom.

What we see in our minds tends to become true. See therefore, by faith, true loving kindness ever increasing in this land, and rejoice in it, giving thanks! This is dynamic; this has power; this will build upon these shores the kingdom of heaven!

To me equality is a dry and lifeless theory. No individuals or groups of people are just alike, or equal. That would be dull, as would any form of sameness. Even all the children in any one family are not equal in brains or stature, or in any real way, but we love them all, and that makes for the kingdom of heaven.

My best friend all the years we lived in New Jersey was Elizabeth, who helped me several afternoons a week. She was a light brown person, lovely to look upon. Later she got a better job, and I saw her only occasionally. One evening the front doorbell rang and there stood a young man whom I recognized as one of Elizabeth's sons. He said his mother wanted me to come. She was dying, he said, of cancer.

So I told my children where I would be, and climbed into the car with him and we jolted over rough roads to the little house where Elizabeth and her husband lived, with some of their nine children. We went into the one large room, lit by a single oil lamp. Elizabeth was in the bed, and around the walls stood her relatives, gathered together for the solemn event of her dying. I could see mostly the whites of their eyes, shining through the dark.

I knelt beside the bed, laid my hands on my friend, and prayed for healing. I did not know how to pray for anything else. Elizabeth knew me, and smiled. Then I arose and was driven home.

Elizabeth, who is about my own age, lives until this day. I hear from her, or about her, occasionally, and if I am ever near New Jersey, she is one whom I would always try to see.

Why do I tell these stories? So that you can rejoice! If you are tempted to put your mind on discrimination and racial unrest, remember Elizabeth, Aunt Adeline, and friends of your own, and rejoice! And rejoicing, pray that the love of Christ may warm and soften all human relationships, and so bring in the kingdom of heaven.

In my husband's New Jersey parish was born the most beautiful and moving Christmas pageant—more than a pageant, a service in song, a processional with costumes and floodlights— a service glorifying the Lord Jesus Christ. Every word of it was from the Bible or from the old hymns. People came to it from near and far in such numbers that we had to produce it twice each Christmas Eve, with people waiting for the second service, sometimes for an hour, standing all around the block. Beauty was there, and the love of Christ, and the joy of His coming into the world. Where His beauty abides, there people will come.

Nowadays there are churches everywhere that celebrate not only Christ's coming, but the coming of His Holy Spirit upon the church and the world. Such churches are called "charismatic." I don't much like the word, as used basically to mean that people speak in tongues in a given church. Nevertheless, regardless of words, where the power of the Lord is, there will the people come. Let us rejoice in this and "see" it increasing all over this great country until the power of the Lord shall cover the land as the waters cover the sea!

As we rejoice we are not hugging to our bosoms a vain hope, but we are simply giving thanks in advance for that which the Bible tells us *will be*. "They shall not hurt nor destroy in all my holy mountain: for the earth shall be full of the knowledge of the Lord, as the waters cover the sea" (Isa. 11:9).

CHAPTER 9

Several years ago I was visiting a friend in Florida and we went out one evening, returning rather late. We came in from the garage through the back door of the big house, and trooped rather noisily through laundry, pantry, and kitchen. Beyond the kitchen was another pantry, no longer inhabited by a butler but by three large cages containing two tiny blue parakeets, two green ones, and two yellow. As we burst into the room, laughing and talking, one of the yellow parakeets, known from here on as Mrs. Birdie, fell from her roost and lay on the floor of the cage unable to move. There she lay on her back with her legs and claws curled up next to her tiny body. As time passed it became obvious that she was completely paralyzed. The little claws became quite black and shriveled instead of their normal gray. She did manage to turn herself over, but refused food and drink, and for several days remained at death's door.

My friend, her helper, Ethel, and I stood in front of the cage and prayed for Mrs. Birdie time after time, asking that the light of the Lord enter into her small frame and bring her back to health. She did, after a while, make feeble attempts to move, propelling herself by her wings, which she used like little oars. Finally she began to take a little water and bird seed, but still could not fly. However, she enjoyed being prayed for! When one or two of us stood in front of her cage, she would shuffle as near as she could get and look at us, with her head first on one side and then on the other, with every appearance of interest. In fact, it became so that if she heard our voices elsewhere in the house she would set up a terrific clamor and squawking until we came and prayed for her. Moreover, Mrs. Birdie's whole disposition changed. She had been the most timid of all the budgies, hiding in the back of her cage if anyone came near. Now she was the friendliest of them all, bustling to the front whenever she heard voices, and calling our attention loudly until we came and prayed for her. She was eating too, but still could not fly up to the perch where her lordly husband sat and sang at the top of his voice. She would "row" herself to the side of the cage, but there was the perch, way up above her, and she could not get to it.

"Oh, Lord," prayed my hostess, "please help Mrs. Birdie get up on that perch!" And He who notes the sparrow's fall took note of Mrs. Birdie, and one day, using her curved beak as one would use hands, up to the perch she climbed. Then she opened her beak and sang, and knew she was a bird; for as my friend and I agreed, unless one can climb up on a perch and sing, one is not a bird! One day her husband desired the whole of the perch, so Mrs. Birdie bit him. Then we knew she was well.

My friend moved west after that, and gave away the three cages and their birds. When I visited her in her new home sometime later, she told me that one night she heard the voice of Mrs. Birdie saying to her, "You forgot your promise." Of course, the Bible would have said that the Lord spoke to her through Mrs. Birdie, probably in a dream. Anyway, my friend heard the words clearly, whether from the faraway bird or from the Lord, "You forgot your promise." Then she recalled that when Mrs. Birdie was sick and showing no improvement, she had promised the Lord that if He would heal her bird, she would stop smoking. She had been neglecting that promise, but now at once she went to work and did stop smoking, to her great benefit and to the pleasure of her friends, with never a relapse.

I have told this delightful, true story to show how great is the power of God, and how small—great enough to enter into the San Andreas Fault and order and control it, and small enough to shine into the body of a little bird who wouldn't weigh more than an ounce or two wringing wet!

> All things bright and beautiful,
> All creatures great and small,
> All things wise and wonderful,
> The Lord God made them all.
>
> Cecil Frances Alexander, 1848

He is the Creator. He is the husbandman, as the Bible tells us, and we are His servants whom He has put in charge of all the wonders of His universe.

I have told the story of a bird in a cage, and now I will come back again to the theme of this book, which is to encourage each one of us to pray effectively for big projects as well as smaller ones. I have already referred to my lady minister friend, whose church is more like a very large prayer group, centered in a garage in the center of a big northern city. She is a duly ordained minister, but has been rather shunned by the authorities of her own denomination because through her the works of Jesus were actually being done! That made them nervous!

Anyway, the area around her church was avoided by most people, since two gangs roamed there before her ministry in the area began. Now, she says, the tough, dangerous young people are not there any more. Some have been converted, one or two are in jail, and others have gone off to honorable jobs elsewhere. From the beginning, that little church has been known to be full of power. Once in the early days a man came running in, terrified, asking if he could stay there overnight. He said that the other gang was out to get him, and he was scared to cross through their territory on his way home.

"You could stay if it were necessary," said the minister. "But it won't be. I'll just pray for you to be surrounded with protection, so they won't even be able to see you." She did that, and the man then walked home right through the haunts of the gang, and no one, he reported later, had even noticed him!

It was from this woman that I learned how to pray for peace in the cities, and I have already told how at a conference where we both were together, everyone was asked to choose one city as a special prayer project, and to continue with it faithfully, praying for peace every day. My friend might have been caught up in more militant protests and demonstrations to obtain needed benefits, but she says that the Lord told her that she was to use no weapon but the weapon of love, so despite all taunts and urgings she has obeyed Him. On Friday nights she and a group of other women have had the habit of praying all night long for the peace of their city. She says that the weekend is the devil's playtime, so their idea was to "get ahead of him"! About midnight they would set up a card table out on the sidewalk, a large Bible open upon it, and they would stand around it with uplifted arms praying for peace. Sometimes a police car would pass slowly, and the women would wave to the astonished officers, calling out, "We're praying for you all!"

That might not be our chosen method of prayer, but again I challenge you who read: choose a city, presumably the place where you live, and pray the prayer of faith for it! Picture God's love shining into it, with the result that there shall be no violence and strife, but that more and more it shall become a center of light and hope for the whole region round about. And I suggest that you tell no one, unless there be one person brave enough to pray with you. Let this be, at least in the beginning, a secret venture. And believe me that this will be the most exciting experience you have ever embarked upon, as you begin to see the results. It is not too difficult to pray in this manner in the United States; I don't quite know why. Perhaps we are not so important to the enemy that he should bother with us. But let us not relax our vigilance, for we are apt to become more and more important in this war of the universe—for that is what it is, or shall become. The Spirit of God is striving through His creatures for the mastery of this world, that it may be saved from evil and become the dwelling place of our redeemer, Jesus Christ, King of kings, and Lord of lords.

There are, however, cities that are more difficult to pray for than those in this country. I think of Belfast in northern Ireland. Have you ever tried praying for that tortured city? Try it, if you feel so led, but prepare yourself for battle! I prayed for Belfast during a time when violence between Protestants and Catholics was at its hottest, and there was a quieting down, yes, but the end is not yet in sight. Surely this strife is one of the knottiest problems that has ever come to the servants of God, for good intentions are mixed up with its evil, and religious zeal with its murderous activities. Indeed, it has often been so during history. If Satan can just get Christian people fighting with each other, then he is well satisfied.

Who is right, and how should these matters be decided? I have no idea, and I do not pray for either the Catholics or the Protestants to be victorious. I only pray for Jesus to win, and for His light to fill that whole area more and more. Thus His own presence will come to abide there, and some day that city will be His. He alone can work out the present differences, welding His people into a unity of love according to His will. Thus His kingdom will come and His will be done in one corner of one country. But this prayer is not easy! I prayed intently during one time when things were at their worst, and now that we do not hear quite so much about it, I have, to tell the truth, slackened up on it. Perhaps the burden is too great for me to carry it alone, or at least I am not aware that others are joining in faith also. Will you help with your prayers? Let us begin again!

Another city, historically important to the peace of the world, is Jerusalem. "Pray for the peace of Jerusalem: they shall prosper that love thee" (Ps. 122:6). But that was written long ago, you will say, and for the Jews. Are we Gentiles to pray for the peace of Jerusalem now? My reply is that we take to ourselves everything else that is written in the Old Testament, especially all the good promises, so why not this? Maybe this was written most especially for us, that we might turn again and comfort His people. "Comfort ye, comfort ye my people, saith your God. Speak ye comfortably to Jerusalem, and cry unto her, that her warfare is accomplished, that her iniquity is pardoned: for she hath received of the Lord's hand double for all her sins" (Isa. 40:1-2).

I do not find it easy to pray for the peace of Jerusalem, but whether or not my little prayers help that great city, I know that they help me. I find therein that peace which I hope some day Jerusalem will find. We always find peace when we are praying according to the will of God, and not exclusively for our own interests.

How then shall we pray for Jerusalem and for our Jewish brethren who live there? Shall we pray that they be convicted of their sins, cease worshiping only Jehovah, and all become faithful Baptists, Methodists, or Episcopalians? You know even while reading these words how silly that would be! Why not just pray for the light of the Lord to fill Jerusalem more and more, trusting that in that light they will see Jesus in God's own way and time? Perhaps they will see Him just as we do, but perhaps their vision of the Lord will be different from ours. One day we can tell them what we see in Him, and they can tell us what they see, and there will be "one fold, and one shepherd" (John

10:16). We need not try to force this ultimate seeing, for we cannot, but in the meantime there will be a strong and safe bridge between us; it will be a bridge of love.

As I have written in other books, there was a time when I prayed a constant prayer, not knowing that it was my variation of the "Jesus Prayer," as an abbot of the Greek Orthodox Church later informed me. The burden of my prayer was this: "Lord Jesus Christ, Son of God, fill me with Thy love and direct that love according to Thy perfect will." During this time I found my love directed toward the Jewish people, and I found, to my amazement, that a prayer for healing for one of these, His chosen ones, worked with more power than did a prayer for any Christian. You may think this strange, but try it and see. I should not say it just that way, for of course if you try it only to see whether it works, and not out of genuine loving concern, it is not likely to work.

One of my first such experiences was the healing of a man whom I will call Samuel Aaronson. It happened thus. His wife sat every week beside a friend of mine at the Philadelphia orchestra concerts. Only a Philadelphian can truly appreciate what this means. Season tickets are usually not available for love nor money, but are often inherited, as some say ladies' hats used to be inherited. I refer to the classic remark in answer to a brash query, during the era when ladies' hats were freely decorated with flowers, feathers, and what not, "Where do you buy your hats?"

The answer was: "I don't buy my hats; I *have* my hats."

Whether or not this was true about hats, it really was as regards tickets to the Philadelphia Orchestra. True Philadelphians did not buy season tickets; they *had* them.

Anyway, one day Mrs. Aaronson came to the concert in great distress of mind. She told my friend during the intermission that her husband was very ill with double pneumonia, and the doctor told her that he could not live. (This was before the discovery of "miracle drugs.") My friend had told Mrs. Aaronson something about me and my work of prayer in the intervals of past concerts, and so Mrs. Aaronson now asked, "Would you ask Mrs. Sanford to pray for him?"

So my friend called me and of course I readily agreed. I suggested that we choose a time when Mrs. Aaronson would be with her husband in the hospital room, not trying to do anything but just to be a channel through whom God's power could flow into him.

The time was set, and we both prayed, each in her own home, for the light of God to come into Mr. Aaronson, burn out the germs that were in him, and make him well. Two hours later Mrs. Aaronson called my friend, ecstatic. She said that at the very time we prayed, the hospital room was filled with a blue light, and her husband was immediately and completely healed.

Do you see? That man was in the direct line for receiving the light. We Gentiles are adopted into the family, but he was of God's original family. The Bible is full of this; in fact, the Bible is primarily the history of the children of Israel who were the children of God. To be sure, they lost this holy inheritance when they did not recognize Jesus as the Son of God, but when we in His name give that inheritance back to them, there must be joy in heaven for there is such great power released.

When we pray for the peace of Jerusalem, then, let us pray with joy. How shall we pray this great prayer? The simplest and most direct way seems to me to pray for the light of God to radiate more and more in the air above that city, and around it, and through its ancient streets. In time the inhabitants will know whence the light comes, and they will look upon Him who died for them on the lonely hill outside old Jerusalem. I need not try to imagine or to interpret all the different shades of feeling that will come to them as they see farther and farther into the truth. I only know that I love them, and feel for them a deep gratitude, for it was the Jews who brought forth Jesus Christ, my Lord—and theirs. Some day they will turn to Him in joy mingled with sorrow that they did not know Him long ago. In that sorrow I want them to know that we love them.

As the light penetrates their darkness, and they recognize the light and come to know Jesus, they need not join this church or that. In fact, I am told that they do not. Many of them call themselves "completed Jews."

So in joy I pray for the peace of Jerusalem. I do not pray for them to defeat their enemies, for I cannot pray for anyone to kill or destroy anyone else. I simply pray for God's kingdom to come in Jerusalem, in the Holy Land, and in the whole of that Sinai peninsula which has been a place of contention for centuries. Imagine, the Israelites and the Egyptians are still at it, after two thousand years. . . .

Armageddon is a small town in the Holy Land. If there still remains a great "Battle of Armageddon" to be fought in that land, then I pray for the light of God to increase there so that whatever battles remain will be finished quickly, and His glory will shine forth toward the establishment of His kingdom on earth.

We cannot go wrong in praying these prayers, for they are in direct accord with the commands given in the Bible—*His* commands. If the Lord saw fit to warn us that there would be great wars and troubles along the way, that was to put steel into our resolve to fight manfully under His banner against the world, the flesh, and the devil. It was not to tell us to haul down our flag and sit disconsolately waiting to be defeated.

But the Lord is coming again, you will say. Yes, isn't that wonderful! He is coming again as surely as the sun will shine again tomorrow morning, putting to flight all the dark shadows of night. But like the sun, His coming forth into full glory may be preceded by a long time of waiting, while His light gradually burns away the shadows of the night. During this time of half-light, of dawn, we are to be His light-bearers, the ones who go before Him bringing the light of His love and power to those who have not known Him.

My parents and many other missionaries have taken that light to far places, and in spite of all discouragements, there it is shone. One discouragement to us in China was the great need for the essential supplies of food and shelter. We had no adequate way of coping with that need, but when a way is needed the Lord opens a way. This He has done through various new forms of missionary endeavor, attempting to teach family planning, good agriculture, adequate care for the sick, education and almost everything man needs in addition to, and fully in accord with, the gospel of Christ. Emphasis is not so much on helping people in deprived situations as on showing them how to help themselves. I rejoice in all such work, and pray for those carrying it on. Also, since I cannot dart off into all the needy countries of the world, or even to all the needy places in our own country, I contribute toward these creative Christian ventures, and am not at all worried that the millennium may come before the money contributed has all been used. I simply rejoice that the use of this money may help to bring the millennium.

Now to leap to another subject, touched on repeatedly throughout this book so that it may really become familiar to us in our deepest understanding, the Bible is full of stories of prayer for protection from wind and storm, fire and tempest, as well as for changes in the weather according to the needs of the people. Most of the time we need not concern ourselves with these matters, for they are in the hands of the Almighty whose power has set the earth rolling around the sun with the winds following its course. Occasionally, often due to human carelessness, a forest fire starts and then the winds become a matter of immediate concern. I have already described how I prayed a prayer of command that the winds should turn about and blow in the opposite direction, when a forest fire near my house in California was not responding to the expert efforts of the firefighters to contain it. I have done this a number of times, always with success, though I find it best not to talk about it at the time because of people's unbelief.

A perplexing point does come to mind, applicable to our use of the prayer of faith in many situations. It is this: if God wanted the wind to stop when that fire was threatening, why didn't He just command the wind to be still then and there? Why did He apparently need someone to stand between Him and nature and give the command, when ordinarily this is not so. He sends us rain and sunshine, wind and calm, without our concerning ourselves with the matter, just as He ordinarily sends us health and strength whether or not we think to pray about it. It seems that sometimes the times are out of tune and He needs us, His servants here on earth, to speak the word of power to wind or storm, or to certain diseases that sneak up on us and on our friends. Jesus did this, acting as God's viceroy. Paul thus officiated in God's name, and so did the other disciples. Moses spoke to the water, and it obeyed him and flowed out of the rock. We can think of many other biblical instances, and there is nothing so strange about this. Did God not make man and put him in the garden of Eden to till and dress it? That is, God made man and put us upon the earth as His overseers to take care of the things of the earth, with spade and hoe, with bricks and mortar and wood, and also with the word of power which has more force than any number of spades, bulldozers and fire engines.

We are to order and control the earth, to make beautiful its highways and gardens, its lakes and rivers; we are to enjoy its great oceans and delight in its glorious mountain ranges. What a trust! He is Lord of all, but we by His decree are His underlords, His trustees, and it is our constant duty to pray for His kingdom to come upon earth, and to help Him to establish it.

In doing so we must consider always what is best for the earth around us and not simply for ourselves. Probably the reason why many people who pray avidly, especially for physical healing, cannot pray effectively for the earth and the world is that they do not consider nor feel concern for any but their own bit of land, and their own immediate convenience. Even in a season of drought, they will pray for continued dry weather so as to enjoy golf or picnics without disturbance. In so doing they cancel out their power to pray for an earth perhaps at that very time desperately needing rain.

To pray for the earth is really one of the greatest joys of life. It is a delight to ask God's blessing on shining fields, or a lovely bit of flower garden. It is an adventure to send God's love to roses and behold those flowers returning His love with beauty! It is a delight to know that a bit of God's light is in one's own garden and in one's own home.

We know the presence of the Lord is increasing in the house and in the land around it because it is constantly surrounded and nourished by prayers. We ask the Lord to bless it, and He does. He pours out His love, and the sunlight of His joy shines upon it continually.

If everyone so prayed for his country, its mountains and seas, its plains and towns, and if everyone so prayed for his own bit of the earth where he lives and where he plants his "vine and fig tree," would we not have peace upon the earth? Indeed we would, and we would have a foretaste of His kingdom.

Do we really want His kingdom to come upon earth? Then if we do, let us claim its coming by faith and fix our minds upon it, seeing it in the imagination of our hearts and minds. Again I repeat that the things that we see in our minds tend to become true. Or do we by chance want a great tribulation to come upon the earth? If so, we can bring it by fixing our minds upon it.

I believe we can go either way. We can go south, for instance, toward warmth and beauty and flowering trees and fruit, or we can go north toward icebergs and frozen tundra and freezing death. Which way do we want to go—toward death and destruction, or toward the joy of heaven and the kingdom of Jesus Christ on earth? We go the way we are looking. No one can look north and go south. Let us fix our minds therefore on life, that we and our children may live!

CHAPTER 10

Once more, coming near the conclusion of this book, I want to turn our thoughts to heaven. After all, if we are in earnest about building the kingdom of heaven on this earth, as Jesus told us to pray, then the clearer our idea of heaven is, the more will we understand what we are trying to do here for His glory. Our concept of heaven, and anticipation of it, has everything to do with our Christianity, our understanding of the Bible, and our obedience to Jesus, our Lord.

Jesus was, in human terms, an impossible dreamer who spoke sometimes with what we can only call fantastic vision and hope. If only He had said something simple like, "Believe on me and be good, and you will go to heaven"! Our lot would then have been very simple, or would it? It would have been bafflingly simple if our only idea of heaven was floating around on clouds and playing harps, because not for very long would that be an ideal existence.

In fact Jesus was not an impossible dreamer. What He said near the conclusion of His life on earth was the most impossible and glorious thing imaginable. He said in perfect seriousness to His disciples: "Go ye into all the world, and preach the gospel to every creature" (Mark 16:15). Yes, I have quoted this before, and perhaps it makes you uncomfortable and you wish I would forget it and get down to brass tacks, like talking more about how our bodies can be healed when we are sick. But I cannot forget it, for there are no brass tacks in His universe, no facts nailed down and solid and completely unexpandable.

The universe has many planets, and there is no reason to assume that this is the only one that is inhabitable. There may be other planets where life is just beginning and where at the moment nothing lives except microbes. There may be yet other planets in other galaxies than ours where life is highly evolved, and indeed where the angels and the saints are way ahead of us in knowing how to rejoice in the glory of the Lamb. And it may be that after death we go in our spiritual bodies to one or another of these real places on real planets, and there serve God in ways that we cannot yet know but which will surely be to go from strength to strength in His perfect service.

Perhaps we will look through a heavenly telescope and see our little planet, Earth, and marvel that that's where we came from—that tiny globe, way down there!

Or perhaps we will look far away to glories indescribable and say, "Hallelujah! There, Lord? Am I really to go there?" hardly believing the bliss of it.

You may be thinking, "Now she's getting fanciful. Why doesn't she just quiet down and tell us how to keep well?"

That is what I am doing, exactly! But there comes a time when it is reasonable to suppose that we will not much longer live on this planet, even with the help of a lot of aspirin and vitamins, and so it is sensible to think of what the next step may be. These are not getting-ready-to-die thoughts. They are getting-ready-to-live-in-heaven thoughts, and while younger readers may want to stop at this point, I am quite sure that some of the older ones may be interested in my wonderings and reflections on the next life. I could gather up a basketful of Bible verses about this, but so can you, and I think it would be more practical to share some of the revelations that the Lord has shown me. I have referred in a previous chapter to some of the later ones, but now I want to go back to the first one of all, when I was quite young, about ten years old as I recall.

In a dream I saw the "sea of glass" around the throne (Rev. 4:6). I cannot describe it, only to say that it was like glass stretching out to infinity on every side. Yet it was not really glass, for it was an essence of life, on and on and on, without glare or shadow. Was it God's light that thus went on as far as the eye could see, the raw material, as it were, out of which the worlds were made? I do not know, but as do all visions, to think of it fills me with joy even to this day. As God's light increases within us, so more and more will we see light and in His straight ways will not stumble.

This was the only vision of heaven that came to me in my youth, but in recent years, as I have already indicated, when I sit down to meditate and lift my spirit up unto the Lord very often I hear the call, "Come up hither!" or to my more earthly mind, "Come on up!" Then I seem to escape lightly from the bonds of my human being, and to live for a while in the spirit in one of the many mansions of heaven. I think this is really quite a natural thing at my age, now nearing eighty years. Apparently the mind becomes wearied or bored with the life that we are now living.

As I have already indicated, I have been many times in the New Jerusalem, with the city wall of rainbow colors merging and melting around its foundations, the gates of pearl, the river of life flowing through the midst of it—just as St. John described it. Surely he had been there too! The golden streets are not hard and solid, like our gold. Walking upon them was more like walking in a golden mist, warm and comfortable. The colors around the foundations were not jewels set into the walls, but were the colors of the rainbow, clear yet evanescent, the tones of them constantly shifting. It seemed to me that where the mystical light of heaven, bright yet not glaring, melted into the ordinary light of earth, there one saw the rainbow colors.

The gates (and I seemed to be aware of twelve without counting them) were indeed exactly like great pearls, mysteriously luminescent. They were not hard and solid, though; they were globes of a shining pearly mist. And I had the feeling that the reason why St. John saw them as twelve, three on each of the four sides, was that each gate was adapted for the final cleansing and purifying of one of the twelve types of personalities, which some psychologists identify. I at least know, as we all do, that there are different types of people, and it seemed to me that the pearly light, or energy, accomplishes some kind of gentle final cleansing as living persons, souls, enter heaven.

I did not go through the gates because, obviously, I am not dead yet. And of course my complete personality was not in heaven in those visions. The visible, human part was sitting right in my study chair, but the heavenly life was for that time more real to me than was the human body in which my soul abides.

Once my angel took me to the verge of the river of life. There it was, flowing clear and cold over the rocks, rainbows in its spray as it flowed in little waterfalls through the meadows. There were its grassy banks, where maybe David rested in the spirit as he struggled through the weary land of this life. Once, only once, and this was rather frightening, the angel took me into the water and baptized me anew into a new life. He went in ahead of me, and I remember thinking like an anxious housewife, "Oh, he'll get his robes all wet!" But they did not become wet, nor droop and cling as a wet garment does. Even in the water they maintained their gentle folds, and when he came out of the water they were quite dry. He led me by the hand into the water and immersed me in it. I do not know just what this accomplished for my soul; I have never bothered much about my soul, but have just trusted the Lord to look after it.

Once or twice I have been in the spirit in quite a different place. It seemed like a great school or library; the light was not bright as in the other heavens, but restfully dim, with a blue or violet tinge. Although I did not see them clearly, it seemed to me that the place was full of books, arranged neatly on shelves, just as we would arrange them in a school library. I have heard people say that heaven is a school, a place of learning. Maybe the one I saw is just such a place!

Again, I found myself in quite a different heaven. It was high and lifted up on the top of shining white mountains, yet the whiteness was not snow, for it was not cold. And I had seen those mountains long ago in a vision! It was when life was very hard, and I felt myself toiling in a small boat over a rough and dangerous sea. Then I lifted my eyes and there before me shone those mountains, far and serene, and I took heart and found courage to go on.

On a mountainside there shone a light, not a static light but one changing continually, now shooting forth its radiance, now drawing it back to the center. I knew, standing near to it in this vision, that amidst the light there was a throne, the Great White Throne, and Him that sat upon it. I could not see Him. I just knew that He was there. From time to time His hand reached forth toward me, a strong, brown hand. Then the clouds of light parted a little, and I saw His face, brown and tender and smiling. Then it was hid again behind the clouds of light.

So much for my little visions of the life to which I believe we are going. We can also, I am sure, have contact with angels while we are yet in this life, without traveling in the spirit to the heavens. For instance, once years ago I stumbled on going up some very steep stone steps into a country church. I felt myself falling backwards; those steps were on a steep slope, and there was no telling where the fall might stop! Then I felt a strong hand behind me, pushing me back to equilibrium. I actually felt the pressure on my back—but there was no one there. Might it have been an angel, my guardian angel perhaps, watching over me?

My husband saw an angel once when he was old and near to dying. "I thought I saw an angel standing in the doorway," he told me.

"I'm sure you did!" said I to him, for if anyone deserved to see an angel, he did. The doorway was symbolic, for not long afterward he went through the doorway to everlasting life.

Will we be with the angels, and will heaven really be anything like the little pictures of it that I have seen? I believe it very likely will, but also that there is not just one heaven, but more than one. "In my Father's house are many mansions," said Jesus (John 14:2), and knowing this I am released from a certain sneaking fear of heaven that I used to have—really a fear of boredom!

Many years ago I read a story in a magazine that I have never forgotten. It was about a man who died and went to heaven. Everything was perfect there, and everyone was sweet and smiling all the time. Once he met his wife on the golden streets, and he thought, "Now we'll see a bit of action!" But no! She also was sweet and beautiful, and sailed past him with only a gentle smile. His heavenly mansion was tended by his guardian angel, and was beautiful and most luxurious; but he wearied of it after a while.

"Do it all over Louis Quinze style," he said to his angel.

"Yes, sir. Immediately, sir!" said the angel, who waved a wand and there it was, all Louis Quinze style, beautiful and perfect.

There was no fun in this! He went out and walked the golden streets, his angel in attendance. Finally he leaned over the parapet of heaven and looked down. "I wish—oh, I wish—"

"What is it you wish, sir?" asked his eager angel.

"I wish—oh, I wish that I were in *hell*!" he cried in a burst of desperation.

And the angel replied, "Just *where* do you think you are?"

146

Our concepts of heaven would indeed be hell to many people: unlimited leisure, everything provided, pink clouds and harps. But it will not be like that. John pictured those who have washed their robes as being before the throne of God, serving Him day and night in His temple (Rev. 7:15). But that does not mean that we shall stand by fanning His Majesty, or run back and forth bringing Him food and drink. What then can it possibly mean?

I have repeatedly come back to this: God is a creator, and scientists who look far into the heavens through telescopes inform us that He is by no means finished creating. I wonder whether He may not send us from time to time to some other earth to tell them about Jesus. (I repeat that I positively do not believe that we would ever come back to this earth. With that dreary theory of reincarnation I have nothing to do.)

I do wonder about the next life, but without spending too much time in wondering, for I well know that when I emerge into that next stage of life, I will be told the purpose for which I am there. However, this concept of a vast universe, with many opportunities for living a new life and serving God in new ways, is to me very reassuring. It gives me a greater incentive to live this life to the fullest, in order to prepare my soul for whatever jobs He wants me to undertake later—in many mansions, many worlds, many heavens, all opening new doors to glory.

So the fear of death is mitigated and softened by the eager vision of the life beyond. Nor is the mere slipping out of the body a thing to fear. I know, for I did it once, or rather it happened to me! It was long ago in my college days, when I had to undergo an abdominal operation which would have been quite harmless, except that the nurse by mistake brought me a full breakfast on the morning of the operation. (It was many a year before I could again eat scrambled eggs!) In surprise I asked if it was for me, as I had not been allowed dinner the previous night.

"Oh, yes," she assured me. I had never before been in a

hospital, and the ways of medicine to me were shrouded in mystery. It was not for me to question anyone. So I ate that big breakfast gratefully, and enjoyed it—for a short time. I was taken to the operating room and given ether, and knew no more until, most surprisingly, I was floating right up under the ceiling, looking down at my body on the operating table. This only lasted for a short instant, much to my disappointment, for I wanted to know what would happen next. But the doctors were down there doing things to my body, and the next thing I knew I was back in my room, feeling very sick indeed. In fact, for several days I was so miserable that I really did not want to live. Do you know what gave me back the desire to live? Not an angel, no. It was a gray squirrel running along the telephone wire outside my window! The joy of life was so apparent in him that the desire to live came back to me! "Well," said the doctor, "we didn't know we were dealing with such a delicate body." But it wasn't the delicate body at all. It was the scrambled eggs that should have gone to someone else, but I could not say so, for it would have made trouble for the nurse.

It is only recently coming to me that these small incidents may have had a bit to do with my fearlessness about death which, I am sure, is not as difficult as we might think. One minute you are here, and the next minute you have slipped out of your body quite painlessly and are looking down at it from somewhere else. (I didn't get very far; I only started on that journey!)

A few years ago in Alaska I met a little Indian lady who told me that she had once died and gone to heaven. It was beautiful, she said, and she did not want to come back. But she met Jesus, and He told her that He desired her to return to earth for a while. She could come back to heaven later, He said, but right now He still had work for her to do on earth. So, she told me, she walked down a long hill. At the bottom of the hill was a little house. She recognized the house. It was her house. It was her body. So she went back into it.

Such little stories, childish stories, yet point to a great fact: life upon this earth is only a stepping stone to the larger life of eternity. What that life will be we do not know, but it will be *life*, not merely standing with angels and archangels and forever singing things like, "Holy, holy, holy." Life is creativity, and without creativity there is no life.

At one period of recent years I noticed myself remembering the early years of my marriage, and thinking much about my three beautiful babies, letting my imagination dwell upon those days. I was once reminiscing about my three beautiful, wonderful babies and my son said, "Mom, I didn't know you had such strong maternal instincts."

"Oh, I don't," I replied. "It is just that I did happen to have the three most charming and adorable babies in the world!"

My son's comment did cause me to wonder about this wandering of the mind toward the past, and it came to me that it would be more sensible to look forward toward the future. After all, it is always best to look where we are going, rather than going forward while trying to look backward!

I remember walking down a dark hall as a very little child in China, being afraid as my little candle drew farther away from the living room, lit with a kerosene lamp. Then I rounded a corner, and there shone the light from the little flat-bottomed oil lamp in my bedroom, and I was once more safe, approaching another light. It would have done no good to scuttle back to the living room saying that I was scared and didn't want to go to bed, for to bed I had to go!

To bed we too have to go, but only to rise out of that bed into the new and glorious light of another world! It will be one of many other worlds; of that I feel sure.

I do not understand these mysteries, and thank God I do not have to understand all about life and death, and heaven and hell. The one thing that I do know and desire above all others is to see not angels or heavens but Jesus, the very Son of the Father,

God of God, Light of light, Very God of very God. He it is who came into this world from all the glories of all the heavens, and suffered and died that we might live. He gathered into himself all the fullness of the Godhead and all the sufferings of mankind so that we, bringing Him our sins and sorrows, could receive from Him God's light. He the light-bearer is also the light-giver. All worlds were made by Him, and therefore in a different radiation His light is within all worlds and in the very earth, which holds its breath in waiting. It is waiting for the manifestation of the sons of God, so that the earth, in bondage because of man's sins—in fact, the whole creation, worlds beyond worlds, and galaxies beyond galaxies—will be lifted into God's glory.

For this, creation waits!